Shipping Container Homes

Blueprint how to build a shipping container home for cheap and live mortgage free for rest of your life

By

Rebecca Simpson

(SDJ publisher)

COPYRIGHT© 2015

BY

Rebecca Simpson

This book or any portion thereof may not be reproduced or used in any manner whatsoever without the express written permission of the publisher except for the use of brief quotations in book review.

EXPLORING THE INNOVATIONS OF MODERN HOUSING DESIGNS OF SHIPPING CONTAINER HOMES .... ERROR! BOOKMARK NOT DEFINED.

INTRODUCTION 13

CHAPTER 1: UNDERSTANDING THE BASICS 15

What are Shipping Container Homes? 15

History of shipping containers. 16

Why a shipping container? 17

Types of Shipping Containers 18
    Shipping Container Dimensions: 20
    Off Grid Cabin 21
    Ranch Style Home 22
    Emergency Shelters 22
    Construction Trailers 23
    RV Campers 23
    School Buildings 24

Evolution of Housing Designs in Modern Times 24

Lifestyle Modification 25

CHAPTER 2: THINK BEFORE YOU BUILD: THINGS TO CONSIDER BEFORE CONSTRUCTION 26

Personal Considerations 26

Greener Environment 27

Permits and Licensing 28

Pricing 28

Right Timing 30

Cost Considerations 30

How much space you need. 33

Transforming a Shipping Container into a Home 34

CHAPTER 3: PROPER PLANNING IS THE KEY 37

Plan Ahead 37

Find a Shipping Container 42
    Online 42
    Local 43

Numbers of Container Needed 44

Purchasing Shipping Containers 45
    Shopping Considerations: 46

15 Tips to Consider in Purchasing Container 52

Materials and Quality 55

Age 55

Location and Installation 56

Floorings 57

Wall Innovation 59

Doors and Windows 60

Sealing 61

Divisions and Enclosures 62

Electricity and Water Supply 62

Insulation Considerations 63

Size Considerations 65

Place 66

Built in amenities 67

Open Spaces 67

Prefab Container Homes 68

CHAPTER 4: CONSTRUCTING A SHIPPING CONTAINER HOME 70

Prepare the building site. 71

Lay down the foundations. 72

Ready the shipping containers. 73

Set the containers on the foundation and against each other. 73

Connecting the Parts 74

Create Openings 76

Install doors, windows, and other panels to cover openings. 77

Install plumbing and electrical systems, heating and cooling systems, insulation, and fixtures. 78

Do a final inspection. 79

Expansion Avenue 79

Tips in Constructing Shipping Container Homes 80

CHAPTER 5: BENEFITS OF SHIPPING CONTAINER HOMES.. 83

Benefits and Advantages 86
- Personal: 86
- Safety: 86
- Speed: 87
- Cost: 88
- Adaptability: 89
- Ecology: 89
- It Is Durable 90
- It Is Trendy and Cool 90

Drawbacks and Disadvantages 91
- Code: 91
- Insulation: 92
- Safety: 93
- Hidden Costs: 94
- Learning: 94
- It Can Rust Easily 94
- They May Have Harmful Solvents and Paints 95
- It Requires a Lot of Space 95

CHAPTER 5: SAVING BIG-THINKING SMALL: GREAT SHIPPING CONTAINER HOMES IDEAS........................... 96

Single Container Homes.. 96
- Make the most of your small space. 97
- Get creative with making rooms. 97
- When you've used the floor space, go up. 98
- Area rugs... 98
- Placing for privacy, and convenience. 99
- All about the wall... 99
- Visual space says it all... 100
- Over and under.. 100
- Less is more, and lighting helps. 101
- Functional furniture, a lifesaver in a small space..... 101

Multi-Container Homes.. 102
- How separate is separate? 102

Vertical verses side by sides. 103
Multi-person multi-unites. 103
Room versus storage: making the choice. 103
Getting the pets on board. 104
Watch those windows! 104
Laying out your layout. 105
Two in one, making the most of furniture. 105
Consideration conservation. 105
Ventilation and keeping it fresh. 106

Choosing the Look that you want 106
The Industrial Look 107
Stacking It Up: Multi-Levels 108
Going Big 108
Going Small 109
Eco-friendly And Natural 110
Making It Fun with Color 110
Not a Container House at All 111
Prefabricated and Mobile 111
Experimental Architecture 112

Container Home Interiors 113

Decorating the Smaller Home 114
Windows 114
Doors 115
Decorations 115
Furniture 116
Bedroom 116

Designs for Living in Comfort 116

Dual or Multi-Purpose Furniture and Installations 119
Heating solutions: 122
Landscapes – Grass Sod Roofing 123
One-Function Container Rooms 123

Saving the Space for Last 124

The Art of Minimalism 126

Storage Solutions that Add Space 128
    Kitchen 128
    Living space 129
    Dining area 129
    Entrance 130
    Bedroom 131
    Closet 131
    Children's rooms 131
    Guest rooms 132

Layouts and Innovations 132
    Multi Levels on One Floor 133
    Staircases 133
    Clean and Dirty 134
    More Storage: Drawers 134
    Racks 136
    Seating 136

Organizing Small Spaces 138
    Tennis shoe flower pots. 139
    Ladder shelf. 139
    Wall china closet. 139
    Door bookshelves: 140
    Boxes on the wall. 140
    Shelves in the cupboards. 140
    Entertainment Studios. 141
    Feeding a small army. 141
    Hollow hallows. 141
    Mason jar candle lights. 142

CHAPTER 6: MAINTAINING YOUR SHIPPING CONTAINER HOME 143

Cleanliness is everything 143

Small Home Mindset 143

Decluttering is the key 144
    Room by Room 145
    Books and Media 145

Kitchen 146
Clothing 147
Kids' Stuff 147
How to Pass It On 148

Maintaining your Container Homes 149
Everything Has Its Place 150
Kitchen Storage 151
Filing 151
Ornaments and Pictures 152
New Stuff 153
External Storage 154
Don't skimp on the services 154
Make sure you do your homework. 154
Placement is key. 155
Windows are made of glass. 155
Keeping your cool when it is hot outside. 156
Don't over plan the work, or the plan. 156
Be mindful of the neighbors 156
Use the proper tools. 157
Keeping it clean. 157
Managing for life. 157

Additional tips to remember 158

Shipping Container Homes, Dos and Don'ts 159
Dos 159
Don'ts 160

CONCLUSION 162

Testimonials

It's pretty amazing to come across a comprehensive guide about shipping container homes. This book is packed with advise, such as it is inexpensive, versatile, easy to build, durable, with abundant supply and most of all its environmental friendly. It involves everything that you need most from the start, on making designs all the way through getting final permits and certificate of occupancy. Great idea with the most thorough and detailed guide you'll find. I came to know a lot more from this guide and after reading it now I am planning to have my own shipping container house. I must recommend this guide to all... **Edward K. Flores**

This eBook seems to cover all the basic information one needs to get started in planning a home using an ISBU. One fact I learned very quickly reading this book is that Sea Containers are now called ISBU's or Intermodal Steel Building Units. Sounds much more professional, especially if one is approaching a lender for financing. The book has some cost data and dimensions as well as structural information that is important to consider..................... **Lawrence D. Dennis**

I've been researching about shipping container homes recently and it's been hard to find a good book. This book isn't very long but it doesn't disappoint. You get lots of information about what goes into building one of these homes and suggestions for different options available. While I would like more details and recommendations for some sections, this author did a great job getting the ball rolling and informing the reader about some of the realities of this process............................ **Ann R. Lewis**

This book is short but has got perfect and quality information on shipping container homes. After seeing many great pictures online, I decided to find more about these homes and all I can say now that I am planning to have one of these sometime later in my life time. After reading the book, I am very clear now what needs to go in and what to expect from these homes. Very good book for anyone who is curious to know about shipping container homes and owning one in future.. **David K. Hardman**

INTRODUCTION

One housing trend that is noteworthy and seems to be here to stay is that of building homes and other working and living structures from steel shipping containers of one or more lengths. The containers form the outer structure as well as inner walls, ceilings and floors. The steel shipping containers are that **sturdy and durable**!

Material things have taken the place of personal connections. People buy these huge houses and then feel the need to fill the house with stuff that is pretty and often times completely useless. How many couches, televisions and tables does a person truly need?

It is time to take a step back and focus more on enjoying life and what we have as far as family and take advantage of this beautiful earth while we are on it. Imagine not having **to pay a huge mortgage** every month while living in a unique and ultra-efficient space? What would you do with that extra money? Maybe you or your spouse could quit work. Maybe you could work fewer hours and free up some time to spend with family, take trips and simply enjoy all the things this world has to offer!

The key is downsizing. Downsizing and getting rid of the clutter is a lucrative prospect also. A shipping container home is one way you can have **financial freedom** and dump that massive mortgage. It is the latest trend in housing as people downgrade their homes and upgrade their lifestyles.

In truth, there is a lot room just waiting to be used, you just have to know how to use it, and we are going to show you how. It doesn't matter if you are living in a single container home or have multiple containers; this book is designed to help you work through it all.

Beginning designer or experienced designer alike, this book has something for everyone. There is no end to the ways you can decorate and make the most of your small space, and all on a budget as well.

CHAPTER 1:
UNDERSTANDING THE BASICS

What are Shipping Container Homes?

A shipping container is a large metal container, which is used to handle, carry and store goods on cargo ships. It is usually rectangular in shape and comes with a large door in the center of the end of the container. These containers can be used to carry an array of goods including heavy duty equipment such as industrial machinery and vehicles to livestock and perishables such as eggs.

Shipping containers are, in fact, so versatile, that they find amazing uses outside of the cargo world. They are used to serve as make shift bank vaults sometimes and make shift clinics. They are also used as stores and on site construction accommodation.

History of shipping containers!

When businessman and ex-driver Malcolm McLean patented the first shipping containers in the 1950's, he was only looking to improve how freight was carried on cargo ships.

Back in those days, it took a week for an average ship to be fully loaded or unloaded since the cargo was packaged in individual pieces. Remembering how inefficient this was and not wanting to apply the same system in his new haulage business, McLean came up with the idea to use containers to carry cargo in bulk. These containers could be handled quickly by crane and would reduce the loading and unloading time significantly. Thus, the shipping container was born.

This innovation revolutionized the shipping industry when it first appeared, more than 50 years ago. Now, shipping containers (also known as ISO containers) are the norm for freight transport around the world.

But little did McLean know that his invention would be used for more purposes than he intended. Because they are inexpensive, easily obtainable, and very sturdy, shipping containers are now being used in architecture around the world.

They have now been utilized to construct almost everything: from emergency shelters and shopping malls to military training facilities and bank vaults. People all over the world have seen the potential of shipping containers in construction.

In particular, there has been an upsurge in the construction of shipping container homes. Architects and amateur home designers have taken up the challenge of converting these steel boxes into homes that are innovative, practical, and even luxurious.

Why a shipping container?

Why would you want to live in a smaller space? In the USA the standard space that everyone wants to aim for is 1,000 square foot per person but this is a figure way in excess of the amount of space seen as normal in many parts of the world where people lack the resources to build even the smallest of homes or steep real estate prices mean that floor area is restricted.

Even in the US, the rising costs of land and construction, particularly in the larger cities, is making the American dream of extensive space and a bedroom complete with walk in closet, full bathroom and vanity for each person increasingly remote. More and more people are therefore starting to look into whether or not they can cut down on excess and fit their lives into smaller spaces.

These containers are built with the toughest of corrugated steel, with tubular steel frames. They come equipped with marine grade flooring and locking steel doors that are vandal proof. The welded seams on these containers are water resistant and they are built to stack easily one upon the other. In fact, when they are stacked together, they offer even more strength and durability.

Along with strength, availability, affordability, and the opportunity to recreate these shipping containers into a home that will withstand extreme weather and the test of time, they make it easy to quickly build any type of home you want to live in. Nothing else on earth offers this many benefits for someone who dreams of building their own home.

Types of Shipping Containers

You might be surprised to learn that there are over fifty different styles of shipping containers available. Not all of these styles are suitable for use in building your home with though. For instance, open top containers which have an open top and opening sides do not have the type of strong structural foundation you need.

Another type of container that you will not want as part of your home is a tank container. These are the large cylinder shaped containers that are used for shipping liquids, including the most hazardous variety. For obvious reasons, unless you want to live in a round home, it would not make sense to invest in this type of shipping container.

Insulated containers, sometimes referred to as thermal containers have insulation, although this is not the type you want for your home. These generally have temporary types of insulation, such as gels. Refrigeration containers, also called reefers have a unit installed to keep items frozen or cooled and these are not the type you want to use for your home either.

Then there are the intermodal container collections of shipping containers. These are the type that are used for building homes. These are also called dry freight containers, cube containers, insulated containers, and ocean containers. If this type of container has a taller ceiling, it is called a high cube container.

The intermodal containers are structures that open from the front only, which give them the structural strength that's perfect for building a sturdy home. If they are dry freight containers, they will not have insulation and are used for shipping dry goods and other types of products which do not need temperature considerations.

You may also hear of these types of containers being called:

- ISO Container, (International Standards Organization)
- Cargo container
- Conex box
- Green Cube
- ISBU, (Intermodal Steel Building Unit)
- ISBU module
- Ocean container
- Sea container
- Shipping container
  - Storage container

The size of the intermodal containers vary in lengths from 20 to 53 feet in length and then 8 feet wide and 8.6 feet high, unless it is a high cube which will be about a foot taller. Remember, the high cube style will have about one foot added to the height, which is typically coveted for having the additional ceiling space.

Shipping Container Dimensions:

- 20 foot: up to 1,165 cubic square feet, which equals about 133 square feet interior space.

- 40 foot: up to 2,350 cubic feet with about 273 square feet of interior space.

- 45 foot: up to 3,043 cubic feet with about 308 square feet of interior space.

- 48 foot: up to 3,454 cubic feet with about 376 square feet of interior space.

- 53 foot: up to 3,857 cubic feet with about 416 square feet of interior space.

Knowing the type and size of container that is best for building your house will become very important as you start to shop for them, especially if you are shopping through resources such as eBay. Remember, you can buy more than one in order to have the amount of interior square feet that you want for your home.

Shipping containers can be transformed into different building structures. Using them to create functional buildings is very cost-efficient and also trendy. However, some people balk at the thought of using shipping containers to build homes. But if designed properly, your shipping container home can become indistinguishable from conventional homes. This chapter will discuss about the types of shipping container homes that you can build.

Off Grid Cabin

Shipping containers are great base to start building an off grid cabin. The best thing about building an off grid cabin from a shipping container is that it is extensible and modular which means that you can easily upgrade it by adding another container to improve the living space. Moreover, you also don't need to include many additions to your off grid cabin and you can just use the existing rectangular design of the shipping container as the structure of the off grid cabin. The benefit of an off grid cabin is that it does not take a lot of time as well as expenses to build your cabin from start to finish. However, since you are working with limited space, you need to make sure that you utilize all space in the cabin to make your home more functional.

Ranch Style Home

A standard 40' shipping container has a total area of 67.5m^3 while a 20' container is 33.1m^3. If you stack 6 shipping containers, you end up constructing a lavish ranch-style house with 12 foot vaulted ceiling, two to three bedrooms, a bathroom, a modest kitchen area and a large living room. You can also build a two-storey ranch-style home and use the existing structure above the shipping container as the base of the floor

Emergency Shelters

Shipping containers can be used to create emergency shelters to provide people with temporary shelter in case of emergencies such as disasters, domestic violence and social abuse. Instead of tents and other temporary shelters, shipping container shelters are better equipped to protect people against harsh weather conditions and they also last for a long time. Shipping containers are very cheap for organizations that are looking for ways on how to build cost-effective shelters for people whom they want to help. They also have sustainable designs to respond to the global environmental crisis. Many countries all over the world use shipping containers are emergency bunkers for people misplaced by natural calamities and wars.

Construction Trailers

On-site construction housings are often built from shipping container homes. Some construction projects require most of their workers to stay on site and building and using shipping containers is very efficient because the structure is already there and all there is to it is to build partitions in the shipping containers, install insulations to make it livable. Moreover, construction trailers made from shipping containers are also mobile thus they can be taken out from the site easily as soon as construction is over.

RV Campers

If you are a serious DIY enthusiast, then you can use a 20' container van and transform it into an RV camper. Shipping containers are ideal for RV campers because they already take the shape that can easily be pulled by adequate flatbeds. An RV camper built from shipping containers can still have the same features of conventional RVs. The best thing about RV campers built from shipping containers is that they are economical as the cost is cheaper compared to buying a brand new RV.

School Buildings

Shipping containers are now used by many organizations all over the world to construct cheap school buildings that are durable and also safe for children. Schools built from shipping containers are not only environmentally friendly but they are also very trendy. They can also be used to build youth centers and other educational facilities where children can get academic instructions. The thing is that there are many types of buildings that can be constructed out of recycled shipping containers.

What makes shipping containers ideal for different types of homes is that they are very versatile. Moreover, their rectangular shape is also idea for constructing the base of buildings as it adds not only a strong foundation to the building but also a versatile shape for possible future expansions.

Evolution of Housing Designs in Modern Times

Whether you live in New York, Chicago, LA, Tokyo, Hong Kong, Paris or London city life is almost universally exciting. Living close to the center of the city allows you to enjoy the very best of arts, culture and fine dining.

Cities might have good transport links but the universal truth is, no matter which city you live in, the closer you are to the center the more likely you are to enjoy the best of city living. The trouble with this is that everyone wants a slice of the action and with as many people as possible wanting to live in the center and with land prices typically higher in the center the housing stock is (unless you have a very large budget) likely to be cramped.

If you want to enjoy the benefits of city life, therefore, you will have to sacrifice space for style. A small space does not, however, need to be cramped and this book will show you how to make the most of your small but perfect city home.

Lifestyle Modification

There are many benefits to living in a smaller home, it might let you live closer in to the center of the city or you might decide to downsize to fulfil your financial obligations at a younger age and therefore permit you a secure retirement. The many other benefits of living in a smaller space include cheaper heating costs and a smaller space to keep clean and tidy giving you more time to yourself during your evenings and weekends. Because you have less space to store things you will spend less of your income on fripperies and impulse purchases and, if you are part of a family, you will spend more quality time together instead of isolating yourselves in different parts of the house.

CHAPTER 2:

THINK BEFORE YOU BUILD: THINGS TO CONSIDER BEFORE CONSTRUCTION

Personal Considerations

Planning is the real key to a build that is efficient, economical, and achievable. Even before coming up with a design plan, there are many factors that need to be considered. Proper preparation ensures that the build goes smoothly when it is actually under way.

One of the main issues with these kinds of homes is insulation and heat control. Shipping containers are basically large steel boxes, so it goes without saying that they transmit heat and cold very well, making it incredibly hard to control the temperature inside them. This can be helped with thorough insulation and the right kind of paint, but it can be difficult to manage and too much insulation will eat away at the already limited amount of space left inside the container.

Secondly, these containers do deteriorate. The idea is to buy shipping containers cheaply when they reach the end of their lifespan, so chances are you'll have to do a lot of maintenance to keep it in good shape. Most are made from 'Corten steel' and will rust quickly, especially if they have been scratched or dented. This can be rectified, but it means you're building a home out of a damaged material – not necessarily the smartest move.

Greener Environment

To top it all, shipping container homes can be way better for the environment, thus protecting our beloved planet. After all, without this planet we would have no available means to sustain human life. For these reasons, a shipping container home is an incredible step-up with regards to human conscious morality and sustainable living.

When not even considering all the other great benefits, choosing to live via shipping container homes is an awesome, and selfless, way to ensure Earth's stable place in our solar system. For you to build a conventional house, you need to cut down a lot of trees. Think about how many trees that need to be chopped down for you to build your dream house. With shipping containers, you recycle used storage containers which is a very eco-friendly approach.

Permits and Licensing

Next is the issue of obtaining a permit. Since shipping container homes are a relatively new idea, it might be hard to get your hands on the necessary building permits in your area. Just to place a shipping container on you land, a permit is technically required. That is, unless you live on farm or agriculturally approved land. The process is timely, sometimes taking years, and might never be resolved positively. Applying for a permit also has a cost and, of course, the time it takes could slow down the 'quick build speed' considerably.

Still, it is a great way to help live a nice, sustainable lifestyle and improve our planet simultaneously – if you do it right!

Pricing

However, there are also a lot of benefits from building in this manner and homes built from shipping containers are becoming increasingly popular for a number of reasons. Their two most substantial benefits have to be the price and the speed. Shipping containers can be bought for as little as $1,200 or occasionally even for free, making them a very cheap building material.

Remember to always offer less when attempting to purchase the containers. Many times the sellers will accept and you can get a great deal on a shipping container by showing interest and bargaining a little. This is especially true for the online sellers. With more money, your home could be more superior, so make sure you don't blindly accept what the sellers offer. After all, getting these for a lower price can enable you to spend more money on design, building, etc.

It is estimated that building using shipping containers costs two thirds of the amount of building with regular materials. This is appealing for a large number of people, as they then carry the potential to be turned into a building worth a vast amount of money. As a building material, they are very flexible and the perfect shape to be repurposed into homes. You can create a small and simple home for as little as $14,600 or plan a more advanced project with bigger and wilder ideas that eventually result in a multi-million-dollar home. This is a craze that is taking off all over the world. One home in Queensland, Australia, which was built using an impressive 31 shipping containers, sold for more than $1 million USD, and there are plenty more of these around.

Right Timing

On top of price, there is the speed to consider. Whereas building a regular home could take a couple of years, these shipping container homes can be put up and built in a matter of months – depending on the scale of the project. It is estimated that construction time can be cut down by as much as 40% by building using shipping containers. In fact, if all the pieces have been pre-cut off site, the build time can be cut down to just a matter of days. It is also possible for a person to build a shipping container home themselves. Most people opt for hiring a design firm and a few experts along the way, but it's perfectly appropriate to do the job yourself if you're well enough versed.

Cost Considerations

Constructing a house from shipping containers is undoubtedly less expensive than buying or building a conventional home. As previously mentioned, the labor costs are significantly less. Also, it is possible to obtain used shipping containers for as low as $1,200 in the United States. A brand new one will typically cost less than $6,000. In comparison, the materials for regular homes (such as mortar or brick) are significantly more expensive.

This is probably one of the most important questions you have. How much does it really cost? This price is going to vary all across the world. If there's an overabundance of containers sitting in a shipping yard taking up space, the company will want to unload them before another set of containers are retired and this will create a bargain deal!

If there has been a rush on used containers (which is already happening with the shipping container home trend) prices may be a little higher. The price is set by supply and demand. Companies selling their containers are going to do whatever they can to pad their bottom line and if that includes charging more for their unused shipping containers sitting on their lot—they will.

There are plenty of private owners who have shipping containers that they want to get rid of. You may be able to haggle with these sellers and get the price down. In fact, there are plenty of sellers who just want these massive boxes off their property and might be willing to sell it at a steep discount just to clear extra space on their lot.

It is difficult to narrow down how much you will pay just for the container. To give you a rough estimate, you will usually find them being offered for $1,200 to $5,000. The size will definitely play a role in the total price. You may be able to get a discount if you buy several containers from a single seller. It never hurts to ask.

Let's assume you are buying 3 containers at a price of $4000 each, which really is on the high side. Your 900-square foot home will cost you $12,000. Now, you can't live in that box as is obviously, a degree of renovations will need to take place to make your steel box habitable.

The following list is additional costs that will incur when transforming your shipping container into an actual home.

- Plumbing—kitchen, bathroom
- Electrical
- Insulation
- Windows

- Flooring-subfloors
- Carpet/hardwood
- Foundation
- Water/sewer hookups
- Electric hookups—unless you are going solar and you would need to install a solar panel system
- Drywall and wood studs for partitions
- Appliances
- Shower, sinks
- Architect or engineer fees—this is a worthy investment and can help you make the most of your container.

Some of these items you can buy used and save a great deal of money. The electrical and plumbing aspects will require somebody who is knowledgeable and certified in the perspective fields. You will be able to do a lot of the cosmetic stuff yourself. The total cost of your home will depend on how much work you want done inside. Do you want a kitchen with numerous counters and cabinets? Do you want fancy lighting? These are all costs you will need to factor in before you take the plunge. The containers themselves are the least expensive part of the whole deal. It is all the little stuff that adds up.

For a 3-container home, you can safely expect to pay under $50k assuming you are doing your best to use bargain shops for appliances and what not.

In the United States, these containers tend to be much cheaper than other areas of the world. This is because the U.S. does not export nearly as many goods as other countries. The cost to deliver the shipping container back is not worth it and therefore, they sit in shipyards for nothing. Many companies take the loss and sell the containers for scrap because of the value of the steel they are made with. The price of steel will influence the price of a shipping container. If a company can make more money scrapping it, they will.

How much space you need.

Decide how much space you need and how many containers you will require. The common sizes for shipping containers are either 20ft or 40ft long by 8ft wide, and the standard heights are either 8ft 6inches or 9ft 6 inches. Extra-long containers are also available and these can measure up to 48ft.

Transforming a Shipping Container into a Home

While there are certainly plenty of reasons why you should consider transforming an old shipping container into your new home, there are some things you need to consider before you jump on board. Nothing in life is going to be all sunshine and roses and you need to know about some of the perceived downsides. However, every downside can have an upside; you just have to be willing to find it.

The containers are sold as-is and typically don't come with any kind of warranties or guarantees. They are made of steel, so there is a very slim chance the container could actually be broken, but people often like the insurance of a warranty.

You also have to be wary of shipping containers that are not made from steel. There are some out there that are made with a substandard material and rust could become an issue. Most containers are made with something called Corten steel and are designed to withstand the corrosive sea air without rusting. Rust is one of the biggest issues you will deal with and a good paint job can combat rust. You will need the vigilance to identify any problem areas before they have a chance to rust and corrode, this could stave off the issue.

Insurance companies will likely give you a steep discount on home owner's insurance because of the durability and fire safety ratings the containers have. This is certainly not a negative thing, but it should factor into your decision about whether or not you want to make a shipping container your home.

You need to understand the size of the container and just how much living space you will truly have. It can be a little tricky to determine when you are looking at an empty shell with no windows or standard man doors. A standard 40' by 8' wide by 7' high will give you 302 square-feet of living space. Some containers are only 6' foot high, so it will be very important you pay close attention to the specs before you buy it. 40 feet is the standard container length, but there are plenty of 20-footers out there.

If you are looking at the total square footage of a container, you may panic a little when you think about the 2000 square feet of living space you have right now. Don't panic yet. First of all, you can conjoin two or more containers to construct a bigger home. It is actually quite common and many people find two to three containers is more than enough space for an average family.

You must also consider the fact that one of the driving factors behind shipping container homes is to simply downsize. You can get rid of some of the junk you have been carting around for years and bring your family a little closer together, literally. The goal is to simplify by shedding the extra weight of useless stuff. It can be a huge adjustment at first, but it is absolutely freeing. You don't have to place so much value on trinkets and omitting useless things can often make you realize that your family and living are what really count. After all, when it is all said and done, the Knick knacks and various materialistic treasures you had can't always follow you around. All you have is your memories. Obviously, you don't need to sell everything but, in my experience, keeping only those things that are really necessary allowed me to embrace a more enjoyable and stress free existence.

When you first go to check out the container or have it delivered, you may be a little taken aback by its outward appearance. They are not exactly pretty. They are not meant to be aesthetically appealing and have pretty paint jobs and so on when their main use was to transport goods. Don't let this discourage you. Think of the container as a blank canvas that you get to transform into a beautiful masterpiece! A splash of paint, windows and some carpet can transform that cold, steel container into a warm, inviting home.

Chapter 3: Proper Planning is the Key

Plan Ahead

If you desire to build your home in an area of inclement weather or near the ocean, then make sure you look for 'Corten steel'. This is a fairly new material often used for coping with weather without rusting. A lot of shipping containers are made from this material as they have to stand up to harsh weather conditions and salty seas when carrying cargo. Because of this, they are not hard to find. They're generally far more resistant to rust and weather so this could be very important in building a strong home.

As with any new home construction, the first step in the process occurs before the building ever commences. However what proves so nice about building a shipping container home is that the bare bones of the structure are—for the most part—already in place. Nonetheless, you will need to create a plan for your shipping container home. To follow are the two main elements that you will want to consider in the planning process:

1. **Envision Your Life in Your Home.** Shipping container homes are often constructed out of multiple shipping containers. By ordering and combining multiple shipping containers, homeowners become better able to create unique floor plans. In addition, combining multiple containers affords homeowners more space.

When envisioning your life in your shipping container home, you will want to consider how much space you will require. Standard shipping container dimensions tend to measure somewhere between 8 by 20 and 8 by 40 feet. Shipping containers also tend to come in different multiples of these dimensions.

Determining the square footage of your shipping container home involves taking stock of the number of people who will be living in the space. If you are a single person without any animals, you may not require much more than a single shipping container. Alternatively, if you are building a multi-person home which will accommodate a number of furnishings, you will likely require multiple shipping containers. Your first order of business is to determine how much space you will need, given how you envision life being carried out within your home.

2. **Establish a Floor Plan.** Once you have decided how much square footage you require, you will want to determine how this square footage will be distributed. Your floor plan will depend both on your design preferences, as well as the land on which you are building your shipping container home.

If you appreciate the idea of an open-concept home, you will want to establish a floor plan that is flat in nature. This means that you will plan for all of your rooms to be distributed on a single level, by laying several shipping containers next to one another. Conversely, you might be a homeowner who enjoys more of a separation between their primary living rooms from their sleeping quarters. If so, you may want to create a loft space in your shipping container home by planning for a second container to be stacked atop the first.

During the planning process, the two most important aspects you will want to consider are the amount of space required as well as the floor plan that you desire. Once you determine how you would like to see these aspects fulfilled, you can get about the exciting step of ordering your very own shipping containers.

If you'd like your shipping container home to be freshly painted then look for a 'factory paint' label. This indicates that the container has only been painted once and will therefore not suffer from the same flaking of paint and rusting problems that frequently refurbished containers will. This is quite important if you'd like your new home to look like a home and have the appearance of something new and well designed.

Modified shipping containers are also available and range greatly in price. Lots of these shipping containers have been repainted or include add-ons such as roll up doors, heating units, air conditioning units, security bars, vents, skylights, internal partitions, insulation, fans and frames. These additions may be a great advantage for building a home and may be features you're particularly looking for, which will cut down the price and effort on your part. However, these additions may compromise the strength and security of the container and it might be better to make these additions yourself rather than trust whomever made them originally. For your home, you want to know that everything is done to a high standard.

Now that you know what type of shipping containers and the sizes that are available, you can begin to consider plans for how to use them to create your new home. There is no limit to the amount of configurations you can come up with in order to create the type of home you have always dreamed of, whether you use one container or more.

If you are interested in tiny home living, then one container will suit you beautifully. This will give you enough space to create either a studio style or one bedroom home. You can then add a bathroom and kitchenette and decorate in your favorite colors and textures. As you have probably guessed, one container homes are the quickest and easiest to build.

For a studio style or one bedroom home, you can use a 20 foot, up to 53 foot container and determine where you want a wall, or walls for the bathroom. You can also choose if you want to keep a wide open living space, or create an additional wall or walls to block off a bedroom. Once you have made those choices, you will be able to know where to cut for windows, if you want them.

Along with having your layout in advance so you can choose where to cut for windows, you will also want to know how and where to run electrical wires and plumbing. Some homes also use gas for heating and if you will be using this utility, then you will want to plan for it accordingly as well.

You may want a larger home and how you use multiple shipping containers to build it is only limited by your imagination, your budget and the amount of land you have. For example, you may put two containers side by side flush against each other, or build three containers into a U-Shape and build your home that way.

Containers can be stacked if you want multiple floors or very high ceilings. You can stack them flush, or set one container to face north to south and stack one on top like a crisscross, facing east to west.

The most important thing to remember is to plan to build a strong foundation to set your home on. A concrete slab is the most durable, but you can also use concrete posts or create a crawl space or even a basement. In this guide, we will talk about using a concrete slab.

There are kits you can buy that will help you create your own home plans. These kits come with miniature containers, grid paper and suggestions so you can build a tiny model of the home before you begin to build it.

You can also download shipping container home design software such as ContainerHome3D. This software allows you to create a three dimensional image of your plans. It has everything you need, including foundation, roof, materials, windows, doors and more.

If you do not feel creative, you can just purchase ready-made plans that will tell you exactly what you need to build any style and size home you like. Some of these plans come along with pre-cut shipping containers and other types of materials you need to get the job done.

Before finalizing your building plans, make sure to check with your local building codes for rules and regulations. Some neighborhoods have strict requirements on square footage and other details that could affect your overall plans.

Find a Shipping Container

Online

Shipping containers can be bought online in a variety of different sizes from a great number of different websites. A popular favorite is E-bay as there is a large amount of choice and there is the option of entering an auction, which could get you a good price. As well as this though, there are many websites dedicated purely to selling shipping containers. It may be worth emailing some of these websites to find out specific details about what they have in the size you are looking for. They should respond with a quote and you can decide if that is within your budget.

You can also check some online classified ads. Many times the savings are huge. Even so, you still want to check out the container before committing to anything. Many are selling damaged, broken, or worn out containers, thus giving you a terrible deal. As with anything online, be as analytical and careful as possible. It could save you TONS of money.

The main thing you want to consider with regards to buying shipping containers online is the shipping cost. When calculating your overall purchase price, make sure to add in the price it will cost to ship these huge structures – especially if they are a great distance away. What could look like a marvelous deal could actually be a money-pit. For these reasons, buying your shipping containers locally could be an easier, and cheaper, method.

Local

If the Internet is not for you then try phoning a local shipping company to enquire about what used containers they have for sale. To save transport costs, try to stick to local companies. Be aware that transporting shipping containers can be very expensive.

Check out your local classified ads for great deals and worthwhile purchases. It could save you tons of money on shipping costs, although you will still need the container transported, even locally. Still, local shipping would self-evidently be much less.

Buying through a local company also gives you the likely benefit of being able to inspect the container before you buy. This gives you a chance to make sure you're happy with its condition before you spend your money. At this point beware of dents, rust and bad smells. These are all bad signs.

Numbers of Container Needed

Once you've decided on the sizes of the containers you require and how many of them you will need, you'll need to get in touch with the local authorities and find out if you're legally allowed to put a shipping container in your desired location. Some places have restrictions on the locations you can put shipping containers. You'll need to check that your preferred location is suitable. You will need enough space to not only build your home but also to have construction vehicles move around comfortably. Also, you will need to find a relatively level plot unless you want to spend a large amount of money excavating the sight and smoothing out the terrain.

Purchasing Shipping Containers

When you have finalized your building plans and made sure that you will be able to get the correct building permits, then you can start to shop for all the materials you will need. While it is easy to find most of these materials at your local hardware stores, you cannot buy shipping containers there.

Fortunately, finding the perfect shipping container for your needs is simple. You already know that you can find them on eBay, and if you shop there, please make sure that you research the seller. This is important because not everyone selling items on eBay have your best interest in mind.

You can buy prefabricated containers that are already cut and prepared for whatever plan you have in mind. Or, you can go straight to the manufacturer. Globalspec.com has ISO qualified manufacturer listings.

Many shipping container manufacturers will sell both used and new containers. Another directory to find container manufacturers is the National Portable Container Association. This association can also help you find shipping methods and custom fittings if you need them to complete your plan.

Shopping Considerations:

Before parting with money to purchase your shipping containers it's of paramount importance to check what condition they are in. Some shipping containers will have been used to transport goods across the oceans for years and years. These will not have a lot of durability left in them and may be structurally much weaker than newer containers. Ideally, you want 'one trip' containers; containers that are relatively new and barely used. These containers are usually made in Asia, used for one long voyage carrying goods to be traded abroad, and are then sold.

These are often listed as 'like new' such as the popular E-bay description. It simply means that they are in good condition and only have a few scratches and imperfections from their singular use. One way of knowing how reliable a shipping container will be is to find out whether it is still 'cargo worthy'. A cargo worthy container will have been given the all clear to carry cargo across the ocean. If a container has been given this stamp of approval then it is still suitable for its purpose and strong enough to do its job. If you really want to make a thorough job, however, then it may be worth hiring an inspector from the Institute of International Container Lessors to inspect your container. They will make a thorough inspection and decide whether the container is suitable for your long-term project. There will likely be an inspector working near the local shipping company you are buying through.

Shipping containers are sitting at docks and harbors all over the country. The lovely, sturdy boxes are waiting for their beautiful conversion into homes. But sometimes, it can be a little difficult for buyers to find the right containers. If you live in the mid-west or northern states, it will be harder for you to find what you are looking for without paying a small fortune due a longer transportation distance.

These containers are massive, so it doesn't make a lot of sense for companies to ship the containers inland and have them sit and hope somebody buys them. Instead, the containers sit in dock yards along the coastlines where many folks simply cannot get to. In some cases, you may be required to have a special license to buy the containers directly from the shipyards. Check local laws to find out what the requirements are in your area.

If you do not live near a port, your best option is to check your local classifieds and Craig's List. There are plenty of people selling these containers. You should include the phrase "conex" in your search to find all of the listings. They can get buried and hard to find if you don't use the right search terms.

Some businesses have realized how popular and desirable these shipping containers have become and have bought them in bulk with the purpose of reselling them to people all over the country. This makes it a little easier for you to get your hands on one, but you can expect to pay a bit more. In many cases it is worth it, because the shipping cost has been covered. Many sellers will offer free delivery within a 50-mile radius or thereabouts.

When you are shopping for a shipping container, make sure you are buying one that is made of reinforced steel. This is what makes these containers so desirable. There are plenty of cargo containers that are not made from reinforced steel and they are not as durable.

Another important factor in purchasing a container is its age. You are going to pay more for brand new containers and containers that have only made one trip across the ocean. Containers that have been used for years are going to be less expensive because they may show some wear. You need to look for rust, which is the only true enemy of a steel container. Dents and dings could also be an issue if they impact the overall sturdiness of the structure. You can use the serial number on a container to get an idea about where it has been and how long it has been in use.

If you can find a container that has been giving a "cargo worthy" seal of approval, you can rest assured it passed inspection and has no leaks. Many containers that are sold as is could be damaged or leaking. It is definitely a buyer beware situation. If you are given the chance to inspect the container before buying, take along a level with you to check for excessive warping bends. Minor warping can be worked with, but if it is too bad, you will want to pass on it. Walk inside the container and look at the walls. If there is streaking, it indicates a leak. If there is a funky smell, it could be the wood substrate. Chemicals are often sprayed on the wood to prevent pests. This can be toxic.

However, because you are going to be transforming your container and possibly removing parts of walls, flooring and what not, the damage may not affect your home. Some sellers will claim the container is wind and water tight, but it has not been made official by an inspector. You could go to the effort of hiring your own inspector. Check Google to see who is available, this can be done abroad also.

Containers that have already been modified with garage doors, housing doors or windows must be carefully inspected for leaks. Anytime you cut into the steel of the container, you are inviting rust and weakening the structure.

Yet another factor is the outside appearance of a cargo container. Many companies will sell containers with company logos painted on the outside for much cheaper than the ones that are plain. You could always paint over the logo or leave it to give it character.

You can also find hundreds of these containers in varying sizes on eBay. Yes, eBay actually has these small homes for sale. Shipping prices will vary, but in most cases, you will be responsible for finding a company to pick up the container and deliver it to your property. Check around and get several quotes before making a decision.

When you inquire about shipping, ask for a tilt bed transportation truck. This will make the unloading process much easier. Shipping containers are very heavy and you would need a crane or a heavy-duty winch to move the container around or onto your foundation. You will likely need a winch to get the container positioned just right on your foundation, but the tilt bed will make this process much easier. It isn't like you and a few of your friends can just lift it off the trailer. A professional tilt bed transporter will be able to place the containers exactly the way you want.

When you are buying from a dealer, they will likely recommend a shipping service. These dealers have dealt with this numerous times and most likely will have drivers in place specifically for this. You could always rent a truck with a tilt bed and drive it home yourself. Compare the cost of the rental and the fuel before you choose this option. The time and labor you put into plus the other fees may not be worth it. Sometimes, it is just smarter to hire professionals to do the heavy lifting so to speak.

You also won't have to worry about securing the load and dealing with any overweight permits and all of that nonsense when you hire somebody to move the container for you. If a little extra effort doesn't bother you, go ahead and do it yourself.

Shipping containers that are categorized as 'as-is' are the cheapest because they are older and most used. Usually they are retired containers because they have become damaged, leak or have issues with rust. These types of containers are the most common and the cheapest. With these, it's likely you can score a good price, but it's true that you get what you pay for. Buying a damaged container to turn into a home could be a risky option.

Well-used containers are classified as 'wind-water-tight', meaning that the seller believes the container to still be fit for usage as it is a sealed, undamaged container, but it has not passed the required inspections for carrying cargo.

If you want new or nearly new containers, look for those labeled "one trip". These shipping containers have only been used for one shipment and will be as close to new as possible.

If you live near the ocean, you will want containers that are made out of Corten steel. This is the best type of steel to stand up to the salty climate in regard to avoiding rust.

If you do not intend to insulate or cover the exterior of your containers, then you will want to look for "no shipping label" containers. They will be painted, but will not have any type of labels or brand logos on them.

Speaking of paint, if you want a freshly painted container that hasn't been refurbished, look for "factory paint" containers. This will help you avoid problems from paint peeling.

You will hear the term "wind-water-tight" which means that the container is considered waterproof and wind resistant. While these are desirable features for your container, it is better to look for "cargo worthy" containers as they have been inspected and approved, where not all "wind-water-tight" containers have that distinction.

Beware of shipping containers for sale that are labeled "as-is". While you may get a great price on these type of used containers, they will often have dents, leaks or other undesirable features.

When you find the container, or containers, that have all the features you want, make sure there are no dents, rust spots and that the doors open and close properly. Also, be aware of odors as even in metal containers, those can be next to impossible to remove.

15 Tips to Consider in Purchasing Container

These 15 secrets are best to keep in mind before purchasing shipping container home plans:

1. Consider taking adult classes on welding, plumbing or electric wiring instead of hiring professionals. Not only will you enjoy learning new skills, you will eventually save money on repairs, replacements and updates. Many community colleges offer classes that teach skills in a semester without having to go through an entire certification program.

2. Get your plans together for what type of home you want to build before you buy your land. This way you can discuss what the best piece of land will be with your real estate agent. Or, if you already own land, double check to see which plans you will be able to get permits for before investing too much money.

3. Never buy a container "sight un-seen". You may not like what you end up and it can be worth it to pay travel expenses if you have to in order to make sure the container you are purchasing is up to your expectations. Also, make sure you are buying from a reputable dealer.

4. Always negotiate for a reduced price. While between $1,600 and $2,000 is the typical going rate for standard shipping containers, you can oftentimes get a reduced price if you are buying more than one. Or, you can negotiate for reduced moving rates to place the containers on your property.

5. Even if you have the plan you want to use for building your home, check it against the layout of the property and make sure each room is placed in the house in the best way possible. For instance, bedrooms should be as far away from the street as possible in order to cut down on noise.

6. Make any other adjustments to your home plans before you even lay the foundation. For instance, if you want rooms with southern exposure, then you will want to make sure to place the largest windows on the south side of your home.

7. Instead of paying expensive rental fees for equipment such as welding or other construction equipment, check with your local community development agency to see if they have reduced rate rentals or even "for free "lending programs for local residents.

8. Buy remnants whenever possible and stay in contact with your local contractors associations to learn about the best deals on materials. You can also place an ad in your local newspaper or Craigslist for the materials you are looking for. Someone who has too much may see the ad and sell to you at reduced costs.

9. When laying the foundation, build out a generous trench and fill it with gravel to make sure you have adequate drainage. For the best results, create a six inch wide by 18 to 24 inch deep trench, line it, and fill it with the largest fill gravel possible.

10. Leave the container doors on. You can fit sliding glass doors in and still leave the container doors on in order to close for additional security or to protect from heavy storms and hurricanes.

11. Use double paned glass to help keep heat in or out, out of your container home. Also, caulk all the windows with waterproof caulk to get rid of any drafts.

12. Use white shades and heavy curtains to help keep container cooler in the summer. Planting trees for shade and opening windows at night and closing them before 8:00 am will help keep your home cooler without having to run an air conditioner.

13. For cold weather climates, use two or more layers of rigid insulation and then use offset joints and a fiber cement protection board to keep the trailer cozy.

14. Consider using radiant heating in your floor boards. Because heat rises, the warm floors will help keep the entire area warmer and keep other heating costs lower.

15. Consider insulating on the outside instead of on the inside to keep as much interior space as possible. Also, insulate all electrical outlets and anything else that you build into the walls.

Materials and Quality

There is a wide range of choices for you to choose from, when it comes to the materials to be used on your house from the inside out. Most common materials include bamboo, wood and cloth and you can also decide on metal. There is also glass and fiberglass and depend on the location, you can opt for the best choice of material.

It is best that you make use of different types of materials as opposed to just one, as variety will help make your home unique. You can buy the material in bulk, as opposed to buying it in instalments, as it will help you get a discount.

The first thing you will have to assess is the containers quality. Although most containers are made of sturdy metal, there can be a few that were made using flimsy sheets of steel.

You will have to personally inspect it or take an evaluator along to help you out. Once you are convinced of its good quality, you can move on to the next aspect.

Age

Container ships have been in business for several decades. Shipping containers became popular in the 50's and ever since, hundreds have been produced worldwide. There are still many that can be as old as 50 years and newer ones, which might be only a couple of years old.

And although these containers can remain sturdy for several years, it is best that you consider the latest one, as it will have lesser maintenance issues. Older ones might have rust problems, which might cause them to crumble easily.

Location and Installation

Find the ideal location. Many states will have certain laws that you will have to abide by, in order to avoid legal hassles. Several governments do not encourage tiny homes, and it is best that you check with yours before you decide on the size of the house. If there is a restriction on it, then you may have to attach another container, to make it big enough to qualify as a medium sized house.

Once you have the location in mind, you might also have to consult neighbors as you do not want them to issue a stay order and create problems.

It is also advisable for you to thoroughly research the area and see if there are other such homes, which will make it easier to set up yours.

Ideally, you must choose a location that is quite picturesque and has trees, a water body or something between mountains. It might seem like a fantasy but why would you want to compromise on the location of your dream house?

Floorings

When it comes to flooring, you can go for hardwood or metal. Hardwood floors can be a bit expensive, but they will give it a very homely feel. But considering the size of a standard container, it might not turn out to be that expensive. Plus, they will also up the value of your house.

It might take a little time and effort from your side to lay the wooden floor but the finished product will be well worth the effort.

On the other hand, you can opt for the metal floor and decide to simply have it painted, varnished and lay a large carpet over it. The carpet can cover the entire floor in your container home and not bother you to have metal flooring under your feet.

Next comes the flooring. Unfortunately, a lot of shipping containers have wooden floors that are treated with a variety of pesticides, meaning you may not be able to keep them. Some experts in the field think of these as unusable and removed them straight away and others don't see it as a particularly big problem. Because of this indecision in the industry, advice is difficult to offer. It's pretty much down to your individual container. If you know what chemical treatments might have been used on your floors and understand the usage history of your container, then this is a great start. Otherwise it's probably best to have them removed anyway.

One method of getting around this issue is to encapsulate the floor with epoxy. This creates an additional physical barrier and prevents the chemicals from doing any harm. To do this, you will need to wash the floors with 91% isopropyl alcohol to remove any surface oils. This will also help the epoxy to stick. After this is done, you will need to coat the floor with low V epoxy. This is a kind of plastic that will not only protect the floors but stop any vapors from previous chemical treatments causing any harm.

If you have replaced the floors of your container, then chances are this step is unnecessary. Still, if you've chosen to keep your flooring, then this additional step might be something you want to consider. If you want to provide an additional barrier between the potentially harmful wooden floor and yourself, then you could add a subfloor. This means you can pour a concrete floor inside the containers on top of the plywood. If you wish to be creative about it, you could even leave this as the finished floor by just adding some dyes or patterning. Obviously this does not offer much in the way of warmth, so it actually might be more suitable to warm climates but the choice is yours. Adding a subfloor does allow you a little more in the way of insulation and can also provide extra height, which is great if you're trying to cover up remnants of removed bits of wall. Of course, you can also make additions on top of a concrete floor as you would with any other property. There really are a great deal of choices when it comes to your flooring, so think about this stage carefully.

At the same time as thinking about flooring, it's a good idea to think about your plumbing. This will prepare you for what holes you will need to create to allow pipes to run out of your home.

There are also the options of having granite or marble installed, which can give your house a classy look. But these will not work as well with the concept of these houses being mobile and light.

Wall Innovation

The inside walls of your house can be done up in any which way that pleases you. It is best that you have it painted, as opposed to wall papered, as paint will last longer and the maintenance will be low. You can go for 3 walls white and one wall brightly colored, to help your home look bigger.

You can also invest in decals and motifs, and make your own designs, if you do not find any good ones in the market. Another plan for you is to take off an entire wall and place large glass panels or one large glass panel. This will give your house a modern feel and allow a lot of natural light to come through. (But of course can decrease the strength of the container).

Doors and Windows

The next stage in the project, if you haven't already done so when you removed interior walls, is to add doors and windows. At this stage absolutely anything goes. You can have French doors or sliding doors, doors with glass or completely opaque doors. You can have skylights or sash windows or porthole windows, absolutely anything you desire (though carving a circle out of Corten steel might prove problematic). It's really up to you what you go for and there a number of considerations that might help you make up your mind. How much light do you want or need? What is the climate like where you are building? How will various openings affect the temperature? Is there a specific look you are hoping to achieve?

These questions are completely necessary when considering how many windows and doors to place. It's better to make these decisions sooner rather than later, as it will be much more difficult and time-consuming if you change your plans after the project is complete, trust me.

Sealing

This next stage can be completed earlier on in the process or it can be done now, but any gaps in your home will need to be filled and sealed. By removing interior walls and structurally changing your home, you may have created gaps between the containers and you will need to fill them in order for you home to be both secure and watertight. To do this, you might need to weld steel strips on the side gaps. You will probably already have a number of steel bars connecting your containers together for support and they are also great for filling gaps. You will want to coat the steel strips in spray foam on the inside too for insulation and further security.

An alternative to steel bars is to use a combination of backer rod, spray foam and caulk. Foam backer rod comes in a variety of different sizes and you will need to choose what is most suitable for you. Once you have fitted the backer rod, you will want you use spray foam to seal it further. Try not to have any foam showing on the outside of the container, otherwise you will have to reinforce it from the outside too using a material such as steel wool. If you leave foam showing on the outside then you are likely to have rodents chewing through it. A great material to use on the outside is OSI Quad caulk. It's a synthetic rubber caulk that will stretch without breaking, can be repaired (unlike silicone) and can be painted, which is often desirable for the outside. This is a great material to use over any problem areas, where you fear your home might not be completely watertight and secure.

Divisions and Enclosures

The next part of the process is to enclose the openings and divide your spaces. If you've had any rough framing experience, then this part should be relatively easy. All you need to do is create a few separate framed walls to fit into the container openings. The good thing about these internal walls is that they do not have any structural responsibilities and are simply used as a kind of divider. These can be either steel or wooden depending on personal choice. The walls are attached to the containers using a combination of screws, bolts, and even some J-B Weld.

Electricity and Water Supply

Now we're getting to some of the more final stages, electricity. The only real difficulty in wiring shipping container homes is getting the wire past remnants of removed container walls. If you have dramatically altered the structure and shape of your home then this may cause some problems but they are mostly easily fixed. If you find you have a problem, you can more than likely fix it by drilling a small hole through the steel. If this doesn't work then you might need to run the wire around the steel and make a custom nail protector for it. This is pretty easy, and cheap, to do and won't be seen when the trim boards are in place so it's really not the end of the world.

Insulation Considerations

Once all the wiring is done, you will want to add extra insulation. Failing to do so will allow condensation to form on the interior steel walls, opening the door to a whole manner of problems such as corrosion and mold. You have the option of insulating the containers on either the inside or the outside, just as long as you do insulate it. This is a very important step in the process. Deciding whether to insulate the inside or the outside really depends on what you want your home to look like. This is something you ought to discuss with your architect at the beginning of the process.

Insulating the outside of your containers is usually done if you want to have a more traditional appearance to your home. If you want it to be earthy and blend into nature for example, some people choose cedar, vinyl and even log siding to insulate exteriorly. Also putting insulation on the outside is a brilliant method of saving space on the inside as your rooms won't be eaten up by insulation. Of course, this leaves you with corrugated steel walls on the inside which have quite a cold appearance, so it depends what you're after. It is also said that insulating on the outside is more efficient in colder climates. If you live in a particularly cold climate then it may be worth doing some additional research.

Insulating the inside of your shipping containers will leave you with a rugged and low maintenance steel exterior and a more traditionally home-like interior. This is one of the most important steps. You want to do what you can to make your home comfortable and safe to be in when it is soaring hot or freezing cold outside. Sitting in a steel box when it is 90 degrees outside is akin to sitting in an oven. You need plenty of insulation to regulate and stabilize temperatures inside your shipping container.

Insulation will help prevent moisture from condensation. When your home is 75 degrees inside and it is 30 degrees outside, condensation could lead to rust. If you use the traditional insulation that is used in stick-built homes, you could ultimately create a vapor barrier. The tiny space between the steel wall and the fiberglass insulation could have a condensation build up. This will ruin your insulation over time and lead to rust.

To avoid that small gap, spray foam is recommended. The foam clings directly to the wall and eliminates the gap. Spray foam is the easiest, but it is also the most expensive. A two inch layer of foam is ideal. Spray the foam along the walls that you have framed. If you are not willing to invest that much money, you could opt to do a 1 inch layer of spray foam covered with a traditional R-19 fiber glass insulation. This will give you plenty of protection while muting sounds from the outside world.

If you built a roof over your container, you can insulate your roof by putting a layer of spray foam on the top of the container. Your roof over the container will keep out a lot of the moisture and the additional insulation will help regulate the temperature in the home.

It is possible to combine the two methods. For example, you could insulate the inside walls but outside ceiling. This will give you more headroom on the inside and allow you to keep a low maintenance steel exterior. However, keep in mind that your ceiling insulation options will depend on what kind of roof you choose to give your home, if any at all.

When it comes to what type of insulation to use, then the best option is without a doubt spray foam. Even though it is one of the more expensive options, the benefits far outweigh the financial disadvantages. You will need to spray a minimum of 2 inches to insulate your container satisfactorily.

And there you have it. After all your insulation is complete and your walls are covered, building is now complete. Congratulations, you have a new shipping container home!

Size Considerations

The process of building your home will vary greatly depending on the size of the project you are taking on. For a small dwelling using just a couple of containers, only a simple foundation such as a concrete base or some wooden supports will be needed. Consequently, for a larger home you will probably need to dig a basement. You will make your decision based on what is structurally required and based on personal preference. It's probably a good idea to ask a qualified builder or engineer what they deem suitable.

If you decide that a concrete surface is the way forward, then you should embed steel plates into the concrete where the corners of the shipping containers will rest. By doing this, you will be able to weld the containers directly to the concrete foundation. You could use walls as an alternative, but again it's down to personal preference. Piers are good as a cheap and easy kind of foundation and they also have less impact on the site. These piers and walls are needed to add additional supports, especially if you plan on removing any walls of the shipping containers. How much foundational support you will need depends heavily on how you plan on changing and modifying your containers. The more changes you make, the more support you will need underground.

Place

For the majority of shipping containers, a crane will be needed to place it in your desired spot. There are lots of other methods out there, but nothing beats the ease, speed and safety of using a crane. Only a small crane will be needed, the kind used for setting sections of prefab buildings will be ideal. Once your container has been set in the foundation it's relatively easy to make any final adjustments with a large crowbar. Try to have your crane position the container as accurately as possible however to cut down on the amount of repositioning by hand.

Built in amenities

This tip is vital when you are decorating a smaller and narrow space that is still quite long. The idea is to not see the space as just one room where you must center everything on one function. You see this in most conventional living rooms where the coffee table or television becomes an altar and all the other items in the room service the use of the main piece. Instead you should see the space more like separate booths of a train carriage and instead of fitting a study and lounge into one huge room, you could corner off a lounge with a literal-corner couch and mount a television on the wall and then have a separate seating area for dinning and then a study further down with its own furniture.

Open Spaces

In a bigger space you often try to hide away a lot of things by putting them away behind closet doors that are meant to blend into the wall or putting certain clothes away into drawers and the like. There are some practical advantages to doing this kind of thing because you might protect them from dust but you can just as easily hide them from use. One interesting strategy is to have all of your storage cupboards or shelves have open doors so that the contents become interesting focal points for the room and you in a smaller space, where you might retain a similar amount of possessions, you won't feel like you are actually living in a storage container.

Prefab Container Homes

If you have no desire to construct your own home or simply don't have the necessary skills or time, you can buy a prefab home. You will of course pay more for this but it is often worth it. Typically, you will sit down with a consultant and go over all of the things you want in your home. There are plenty of different designs and some companies will create custom designs specifically tailored for your needs. You will have the option of having a single container or multiple containers for your home. There are several companies that offer this service so look around and don't settle down for the first good deal you find.

The company will do all of the cutting and reinforcing at their shop. They then ship the containers directly to your property and begin the setup. Each company will vary when it comes to the foundation requirements. You will need to hire somebody to pour your foundation. Pier-post foundation is an option, but you will need to check with your local building codes. These are easily found on the internet and local prefab constructors already know all of these requirements.

The company will go about putting your home together, but you will likely be left to take care of all of the cosmetic additions like painting, connecting your electricity to the power grid and hooking up the plumbing fixtures. The prefab homes eliminate the need for you to hire various contractors to take care of the items we listed above. Your job will simply be to add the finishing touches!

Most people find that once a prefab home has been delivered and set up, it takes about 30 days or so to take care of the rest. Many people prefer this route because they don't have to worry about every little detail, but still get the opportunity to be involved in the building process. If you like to do everything by yourself and are an avid do-it-yourselfer, than transforming a shipping container into a livable home can be the ultimate project for you to undertake.

One company offers a beautiful and modern, 6 containers, 2000-square foot, and 3 bedroom two bath home for around $120k. This isn't bad considering what it would cost for you to build your own storage container home with just one or two containers. Of course, you will need to factor in shipping costs but still, prefab is not a bad option.

Chapter 4: Constructing a Shipping Container Home

The design is ready, permits have been obtained and submitted, and materials and equipment have been ordered. Once these preparations are complete, it is time for the build to get under way. This is a crucial stage, where the project leaves the confines of pen and paper and the actual shipping container home is materialized.

Building a house is by no means an easy task. Things won't always go according to plan and at some point the build *will* encounter problems, but that is true for all construction projects. Don't panic and don't stress.

Even if a third party, such as a general contractor, is doing the work, get involved. Ask how things are going and check out the site from time to time. Following along these guidelines will help keep things on track.

Prepare the building site.

Preliminary work on the building site includes the excavation and grading for the foundation and utilities like electrical, water, and gas lines. Depending on the design, additional preparation might be necessary. Storm water management systems and septic systems are a few common additions.

If this is your first experience with a shipping container home, you may not feel that securing a foundation for this home is terribly pressing. This is because many homeowners tend to think of shipping container homes as somehow different—structurally—than their traditional counterparts. This, however, is a misconception.

The second tip that you will want to implement when building your shipping container home is that of laying a solid foundation. If you do not take pains to lay a strong foundation for your shipping container home, you will come to regret this inattention. You have several options when it comes to laying your foundation. While some homeowners opt to build a slatted wood foundation for their shipping container homes, a more durable and lasting material is concrete. While concrete tends to be slightly more expensive than wood, it is well worth the additional cost.

Before laying the concrete foundation for your home, you will want to clear your outdoor space. Doing so is relatively simple. Go through your plot of land and clear it of any and all debris. This is something you might do all by yourself on a sunny afternoon. You can also go about purchasing your own steel plates. These plates will be embedded within your concrete foundation, in and around the corners of your structure. While these two aspects of the project can be done by yourself, you will need a professional to help you pour your concrete foundation. He or she will excavate the requisite amount of soil from beneath your home, and fill this space with concrete.

Lay down the foundations.

The type of foundation is also dependent upon the design. In general, concrete is used as foundation for shipping container homes. This can be poured or placed as premade blocks. Precast panels are also available from factories, many already insulated, water proofed, and ready to use.

The process of laying the foundations is similar to that of conventional construction. Lines for utilities are laid at the base, foundation walls are filled, soil is compacted on top, a layer of gravel is added, rebar is set in place, and a slab of concrete is poured out.

Ready the shipping containers.

Shipping containers need to be modified before they can be used for home construction. As mentioned in previous chapters, the expense of steel construction is higher than that of wood or others. To mitigate the cost, it is advisable to have as many modifications done off-site as possible. Re-sellers of shipping containers usually have facilities that can make modifications.

Although shipping containers are much stronger than materials for most homes, making alterations to the structure can compromise its integrity. Cutting holes and removing parts can cause it to weaken.

To avoid safety hazards, be sure to consult an architect or structural engineer on the level of modification. Some reinforcement may be necessary to stabilize the structure.

Set the containers on the foundation and against each other.

Once the foundation and the containers are ready, it is time to put them together.

Containers will need to be crane-lifted on the foundation one by one. They are then hooked in place and the bottom corners are welded to the foundation to keep the structure secure. Metal plates are embedded into the foundation to provide areas of attachment for the containers.

Depending on how they will be arranged or stacked, these containers will also be welded to each other. The corners are the strongest part of the container, so it is best to weld these areas together as much as possible for maximum stability.

Connecting the Parts

At this point, you have a blueprint of your shipping container home as well as a solid foundation on which to build it. If you have decided that your home is to consist of more than one shipping container, you will need to make sure that all of your home's parts are connected together in a secure fashion. Think about this step as being analogous to snapping together the pieces of a Lego home: Only on a much larger scale.

First, you will need a crane to assist you with placing your shipping containers on top of your foundation. Be sure that the placement of your containers respects the blueprint of your home. After all, once these containers have been connected to one another, it becomes incredibly challenging to shift and alter their position.

For homeowners who are hoping to connect their containers themselves, they will likely do so by way of heavy duty bolts and screws. If you are not incredibly builder-savvy, you will want to invest in industrial sized clamps that are intended specifically for the purpose of connecting shipping containers together. An apt example of these industrial sized connectors are Tandemloc horizontal connectors, and can be purchased at a number of different hardware stores.

If you are amenable to having someone help you connect your shipping containers, you can easily hire a handy person to weld these steel structures together. This is actually a really simple procedure that can be completed within the span of an afternoon. Again, you will want to be confident about the floor plan. After all, welding your containers together is as close to a permanent home procedure as you can commit.

Create Openings

Although many people appreciate the industrial aesthetic of shipping container homes, these structures still require both doors and windows. After all, a house is completely non-functional without thresholds through which to exit and enter. Furthermore, window openings are essential for promoting an eco-friendly, and naturally bright home. We can place both of these features under the category of 'openings' within your home. This category might also include openings and passages between your multiple shipping containers.

You can go about creating openings in your home in a number of different ways. Indeed, the steel of your shipping container can be cut by any number of the following tools: cutting torches, plasma cutters, steel grinders, or jig saws. The tool that you end up using to create openings in your home will depend on what kind of opening you are trying to create. For example, if you are creating a small opening for your chimney you may want to use a jig saw. This tool is surprisingly effective and allows for precise maneuvering. If you are removing an entire metal wall, however, you will want to use a plasma cutter. Be sure that you don the correct protective gear when doing so: Including protective glasses and heat-proof clothing. Using a plasma cutter to remove walls, between rooms, is an excellent way of creating an open concept home.

After you decide on the placement of your doors and windows, and actually cut through the metal of your shipping container, you will need to frame out these openings. Framing out your doors and windows is a relatively simple process. You will need plywood and nails to create a wooden frame that will sit flush, within the metal opening of your home. Next you will simply slide windows into these openings, secure with screws, and seal any remaining space. Installing doors tends to take a bit more know-how and most designers recommend hiring a general contractor to help you with this venture.

Creating openings in your shipping container is essential for taking it from a house to a home. Opening up your space makes your shipping container more livable; and, doors and windows truly make these structures appear like beautiful quaint and minimalist homes.

Install doors, windows, and other panels to cover openings.

The first thing to do is to measure and cut the openings where doors and windows will be placed. As much as possible, these should be done off-site, however they can be done on-site if necessary. These openings should be framed with hollow rectangle steel sections to prevent them from weakening the structure. A steel L section can also be used.

This is not limited to doors and windows. Other additional openings, such as skylights, should be treated in the same fashion as well.

Install plumbing and electrical systems, heating and cooling systems, insulation, and fixtures.

When the overall structure is set up, it is time to get to work on the interior of the home. Installing electrical wiring, plumbing, and heating and cooling systems are pretty much the same in a shipping container home as it is in a conventional one.

For insulation, a high-performance, four-part ceramic isolative coating called super herm is recommended. It is sprayed on both the inside and outside walls of the container to protect it from extreme fluctuations in temperature.

Drywall is applied to the inner walls and as interior partitions. Additional vertical supports may also be added. Install any additional fixtures.

Once this is done, the house is basically finished!

Do a final inspection.

After everything is finalized, inspect the result with the contractor and a building official. Check *everything*, from the foundation to the architecture, to the plumbing and electrical systems and even the grade and landscaping around the home. This is an important step, because it is much easier to remedy any errors sooner rather than later.

The approval of a building official will be necessary in the application for a Certificate of Occupancy.

By the end of this process, a house will have been produced from steel boxes that were previously only used to carry and transport various things. Now, all it needs are occupants to turn it from a house into a home.

Expansion Avenue

When you decide on your location and have your container installed, you must bear in mind that you might have to expand it later. In keeping that aspect in mind, you must place the container with enough space around it. You might also have to consider the roof of your container.

It should be sturdy enough to hold another container on top, in case you plan to make a duplex house. You must also keep your family in mind and if you wish to start a family, you must have space ready to make another room.

Tips in Constructing Shipping Container Homes

The following secrets will come in handy if you are aware of them before you start constructing your steel container home. This way you can build them into your planning:

1. Before doing any construction, have the containers professionally cleaned. If they had been treated with poisons to keep pests away, or hauled dangerous materials such as asbestos, it is best to count on professionals to remove every last trace of residue.

2. When cutting out the long sides of the container, make sure you add supporting elements such as beams to keep the structure strong.

3. Keep the metal from the parts of the container that you cut out. You can use them later in a variety of ways, such as framing them in wood and using them for a deck or patio wall. You can also use them inside to create shelving or outside to create an awning or gardening containers.

4. Create shelves underneath each step of a staircase and underneath the staircase to maximize the use of space when building a two story container home.

5. Use PEX instead of rigid plumbing PVC for plumbing. It holds up better and can easily be bent by heating it up.

6. For an ultra-modern look, sandblast the paint from the inside of the container and allow the bare steel to develop a patina. This should be done before you do anything else because it will be much easier to clean the mess up.

7. Using old barn wood can help soften the hardness of stainless steel in the bathroom if you prefer more traditional styles.

8. Consider adding solar panels as an alternative energy source.

9. Choose an energy efficient toilet and other plumbing accessories to help save water.

10. Bamboo plywood is sustainable and can be used for flooring and for paneling if you do not want container exposed interior walls.

11. Use a plasma cutter to cut out the windows and door frames. It melts the metal along with cutting and you don't have to replace the parts as often as you do with other types of cutting tools.

12. Really consider the plan you choose and do not be afraid to change it around to better fit your lifestyle. For instance, if the kitchen layout is not to your liking, it is easier to change before you run the plumbing and electrical lines than trying to change it after the fact.

13. If you get stuck doing it yourself, see if you can barter services with someone else in your area who is building a storage container home.

14. If you cut off the top of the storage container to add a different type of roof, make sure you have framing for ample support for the additional weight of whatever type of roof you add.

15. Memorize all the measurements from zero to one inch, down 1/16 because everything you will be cutting will have to be extremely accurate. This will save a great deal of time and frustration from having to stop and count or convey to your building partner if you have one.

Chapter 5: Benefits of Shipping Container Homes

There are a number of personal and not so personal benefits for choosing to build your home using shipping containers. You may be a bit curious about why they are not being more widely used, or why they are suddenly becoming such a hot trend in architectural circles.

Shipping containers didn't come into existence until the 1950s. At that time, they were strictly for the use of making worldwide shipments between railroad, ships and tractor-trailers more efficient. The containers made it possible to quickly load and unload the contents from one mode of transportation to the next, without having to load and unload the contents they contained.

Over the next thirty years, these innovative shipping containers would gain heavier use as trade globalization increased significantly. These containers were built to withstand the brutal salty ocean climate while safely transporting up to 20 tons of products, from China to America and everywhere in between.

The structure of these containers has to withstand being lifted into a ship, off of a ship, onto and off of a rail car, and onto and off of a tractor-trailer, while they are filled to capacity. At the same time, the containers need to protect the contents from any type of damage. Because of this type of heavy use and requirements, they are some of the strongest structures built.

By 1999 there were more than 200 million shipping containers traveling to various locations. The average lifespan for use of these containers for shipping purposes is up to 8 years, with most of them being retired after two to three years. What this means today is that that millions of shipping containers are filling up stockyards all over the world.

Of course shipping containers can be recycled, but the energy needed for this is immense. Instead, if they can be upcycled, or value-cycled into providing housing, offices, and other types of buildings, then energy is saved and the ideal structure becomes available for even the most treacherous climates.

No other structure is known to withstand hurricanes, tornadoes and other dangerous weather conditions the same way that shipping containers are able to. They are also waterproof and unsusceptible to pests such as termites. They also won't break down as easily as brick and mortar buildings do after many years of being exposed to the elements.

Because there are so many millions of empty shipping containers overflowing stockyards and seaports, they are readily available for use. And, because of the supply and demand equation, they are very affordable for anyone who wishes to purchase them.

These containers are built with the toughest of corrugated steel, with tubular steel frames. They come equipped with marine grade flooring and locking steel doors that are vandal proof. The welded seams on these containers are water resistant and they are built to stack easily one upon the other. In fact, when they are stacked together, they offer even more strength and durability.

Along with strength, availability, affordability, and the opportunity to recreate these shipping containers into a home that will withstand extreme weather and the test of time, they make it easy to quickly build any type of home you want to live in. Nothing else on earth offers this many benefits for someone who dreams of building their own home.

If you are still undecided about whether to build a container home, perhaps as opposed to purchasing a traditional home or a condominium apartment, looking at some advantages and disadvantages of a shipping container home may help you decide.

As we present these advantages and disadvantages, we assume that you are going to be building your shipping container home from scratch on your own (whether with or without assistance).

Very often, the benefits and disadvantages of building and living in your own container home are similar or related to the benefits and drawbacks of using one or more shipping containers to build an unheated workshop, barn or any type of large walk-in storage or working facility on your land.

The benefits and disadvantages of building a multi-container home are similar to building a tiny container home – that is, a home from a single container of whichever size you choose.

Benefits and Advantages

Personal:

Personal satisfaction of building something durable and strong, and of value and functionality, with your own hands

Looking for a business idea? There is a potentially viable big business for the right entrepreneur in creating living modules which are ready to go and be transported anywhere in the country

The high surplus of empty shipping containers is just waiting to become a home, office, apartment, school, dormitory, studio, emergency shelter, and everything else you as a business can think of offering

They can be tricked out, transported as ready-to-live-in "mobile apartments" to any prepared cement foundation, allowing a business to develop an inventory to meet demand quickly

You can be a designer/builder of many creative types of homes for clients who do not have skills or desire to do it themselves

Safety:

Quickly get a lockable and enclosed space that is hard for thieves to haul away

Fire-proof shell – steel does not burn or melt at usual temperatures

Even on a geologically difficult site location or a location with harsh summer/winter weather conditions – the containers' heavy weight and durability help them weather high-risk areas like hurricane and earthquake regions, especially when several of these heavy containers are welded together as one (heavier) unit

Ocean cargo containers are structurally designed out of steel for rough handling, heavy loads, as well as harsh climate conditions – perfect for the exterior of your new home

Speed:

Quickly set up an unheated nonliving protected space, such as a workshop or walk-around personal storage/warehousing facility (for large vehicles, over-sized equipment and tools, etc.) with one or more containers, while retaining the ability to customize the outer look, the inner design and amenities

Shipping containers are the outer shell of your home; they can be purchased and shipped to your land plot, all within a couple of days, depending on where you live, and placed on your cement foundation and footings in minutes

These homes can be completed and made live-in ready in two weeks to two months

Cost:

If a shipping company gets storage containers from overseas, they don't usually ship it back to its origin. In fact, it is cheaper to buy a new storage container thus many shipping yards are filled with empty containers just sitting there collecting dust. Since shipping companies really do not have any use for empty containers, you are doing them a favor by taking empty shipping containers off their hands. You can buy an empty shipping container for less than three thousand dollars or you can practically have it for free if you know how to negotiate.

There is a readily-available surplus of shipping containers (as we have said, there are mountains of them sitting around) so according to the law of supply and demand, they are cheap to purchase (from free to about $3000 – depending on size and general condition)

Concrete foundations for such homes are cheap and easy to create without much assistance

Save money on the cost of a building or buying a traditional house with the same functional spaces, surface, light, and amenities – container homes are often live-in ready at 10% or less of a traditional home cost

Many shipping containers have been abandoned or simply parked in many of your local truck yards – call up local trucking companies to see if they have any for sale (or for free, if you just haul it away for them)

Adaptability:

Mobility – create them on wheels under a free-floating roof and you can pull the trailer and container out if you choose to remain mobile.

They are readily off grid, but can be on grid as easily as any other structure.

They are adaptable and appropriate to most climates.

You can create inner living spaces between containers (whole over-sized rooms or interior walkways, indoor greenhouse, etc.) as well as within them, by creating a roof over the entire structure.

They are a cheap solution for seasonal living – a small "cottage" in the mountains or fishing cabin at the lake – for which you do not require a full-sized home.

Almost all commercial sidings can be attached to the exterior or interior of a steel container frame.

Ease:

Building permits are not required if you build your container home on wheels (on a trailer or similar mobile structure) which make the home demonstrably mobile.

Ecology:

For you to build a conventional house, you need to cut down a lot of trees. Think about how many trees that need to be chopped down for you to build your dream house. With shipping containers, you recycle used storage containers which is a very eco-friendly approach.

Steel is highly recyclable: if you're eco-conscious, you will be in harmony with your beliefs to use a steel container as the basic structure of your home.

You can have a greenhouse for all your plantations right in the heart of your home by installing a glass ceiling over an unconstructed space.

It Is Durable

Just because shipping containers end up sitting in container yards after being used once or twice does not mean that they are no longer durable. Shipping containers are designed to keep things safe against the elements. Moreover, shipping containers are very strong when it comes to vertical loads and you can stack 9 of them and it will never collapse.

It Is Trendy and Cool

Building a storage container home is very cool and trendy. It makes a very strong statement towards other people. It exudes practicality, creativity and even boldness which not all homeowners are ready to embrace. If you build a shipping container house, you will be the talk of your neighborhood.

There are many advantages of using shipping containers as basic structures for homes. Hopefully these advantages will encourage you to construct a shipping container home for your next construction project.

Drawbacks and Disadvantages

Code:

Given the US Uniform Building Code and local zoning laws (variable across the US and in each country), you probably need an architect schooled in these laws to design (provide a blueprint) for your structure.

You need to do a lot of local research when you have chosen a plot of land for your container home, in order to be sure that local zoning laws allow such structures (steel homes; this type of "pre-fab" home, etc.)

Many people and communities judge a container home to be "unsightly" from the exterior, and you may have negative critics to deal with.

Building permits still require (in most US states) the stamp of approval of a structural engineer or architect if you are setting your container home on a permanent foundation.

Many residential areas restrict the types of homes that can be constructed within a particular area. Steel homes, for instance, are not commonly built in residential neighborhoods and you might face serious problems when applying for a building permit within a residential zoning. To remedy this, consult with your local authorities and make sure that your shipping container home will meet all local building codes.

Insulation:

Condensation problems inside the container need attention in the home design stage and must be dealt with during the early build-out phase.

Shipping containers are made from metal (either steel or aluminum) thus it can conduct heat very well. If you build a shipping container home, the temperature can easily get too low during cold season and too unbearably hot during the hot season. However, this can be easily solved if proper control of temperature is installed.

They have been shown to be viable in all climates, with the caveat that in very low-temperature winters and high-temperature summers, insulation must be appropriate to the needed thermal efficiencies – at extra cost to you.

Steel (and the aluminum containers as well) are excellent heat conductors, which essentially means that in winter the structure gets much colder than the external temperature, while in the summer heat, the structure gets much hotter than the outside temperatures.

Although there are some engineering challenges, related to cutting windows and doors and other openings in the side of the containers, and related to stacking and welding them in various obvious or creative ways – these are quickly overcome with a little forward planning … and the correct tools.

Safety:

Rust – try to get containers with no rust, as treating rust is a cost that you just don't need for such economical housing.

As sea-going containers were never meant as human living structures, we just may never know what sort of hazardous materials have been used in their manufacture (paint or rust-reducing chemicals).

Likewise, we never know what sort of hazardous materials (with what type of toxicity to humans) any given shipping container has transported and if there was any seepage into the structure.

You will need to discard any wood flooring of your purchased container to avoid contact with residual chemical spills.

You might need to have the inside and outside professionally "washed" to remove all chemical residues from the steel (Grade A may be an exception, but be cautious).

A very small land plot may seem economical at first, but not allow you enough space to place the container (maneuvering room for the transport truck, etc.) or for your building team to move around the container or containers to modify and build out the home.

Hidden Costs:

Shipping containers are only the outer shell of your home – the rest of the building materials and purchase of land are the bulk of your cost.

You'll need to plan ahead and blueprint the design.

From the design and chosen materials you create a viable budget.

Learning:

If choose, but are not used to, an off-grid home or composting toilets, you may have a learning curve that is uncomfortable for you.

If you are not used to "pod" living – that is, one shipping container for each functional room – you'll also have a learning curve in that sort of design.

It Can Rust Easily

Most shipping containers that are available today are categorized as Intermodal Steel Building Units (ISBU) which rusts easily. If you are looking for a good quality shipping containers to build your home, look for containers that come with weather resistant paints. You can also reinforce recycled shipping containers by applying a fresh coat of weather-resistant paints to make them last longer.

They May Have Harmful Solvents and Paints

Some manufacturers of shipping containers coat the containers with harmful paints as well as solvents. Breathing these substances can be harmful to health. Moreover, some shipping containers carry many types of goods including dangerous chemicals and even radioactive materials. Spillage of these goods may leave contaminants in the shipping container. It is very important to check what types of goods were stored in a shipping container before you decide to use them to build shipping container homes.

It Requires a Lot of Space

Container homes are fairly large and they require enough space for handling during the construction process. If you are planning to build a shipping container home, make sure that you have enough space for your new home.

The thing is that shipping container homes are not perfect and knowing the different pitfalls of shipping container homes allows people to mitigate solutions to the possible problems of this type of home.

Chapter 5: Saving Big-Thinking Small: Great Shipping Container Homes Ideas

Single Container Homes

Some people like to build their shipping container homes to grand sizes, using as many as they can to make almost mansion size houses out of these simple little shipping containers.

While that may be a dream for you one day, if you only have a single unit home right now, don't be discouraged, you can still make a fantastic home, and in some ways, smaller units are better. They are easier to keep clean, less expensive in a lot of ways, and you just get that all around cozy feeling.

There is nothing wrong with having a single unit container home, and we are going to show you how you can have one and decorate it into a fun and quaint little home, perfectly suited for your needs.

Make the most of your small space.

People tend to go one of two ways with their small spaces. Either they barely decorate feeling that they don't have enough room, or they over decorate, thus resulting in a cluttered and over-crowded room.

When you are decorating, make sure you use the space that you have, but that you maintain an organized atmosphere. You will make your guests feel more welcomed when you do, and you will be able to find things and easily move about your home.

Get creative with making rooms.

There are many ways you can make rooms. You can either: go studio style and have a really open floor plan, which tends to work best if you are single or if you are only there with your significant other, or you can make rooms.

If you choose to make rooms, you again have a choice, you can make actual solid rooms out of wood, or you can simply use room dividers. While this is entirely up to you, we like the idea of the room divider, it makes decorating and redecorating so easy, and you can move an entire room if you so choose. There is so much freedom in this way of doing things, why not embrace it?

When you' ve used the floor space, go up.

Floor space gets eaten up quickly, and that is especially true when you are in a small area. Make sure you use all areas that you can, without making the room cluttered. When you have used the floor, it is time to head for the ceiling.

Use the wall as much as you can, and employ the ceiling often. If you don't know where to put something on the ground, then use the ceiling!

Rafters, hooks, and even suspended furniture are all ways you can free up your floor space while still making the most out of storage. Beds are easily hung from the ceiling, especially when the ceiling is as firm as the shipping container ceilings are.

Area rugs.

All of the metal in a shipping container home makes it noisier than conventional homes, this is a problem that can be easily fixed though. The fastest way to do this is to lay down area rugs.

You can also install carpeting, but, as we have said with the walls, it is easier to do something that you can change if you want to, so why not go with the freedom of an area rug?

An added benefit: you can change them out to go with the seasons as well.

Placing for privacy, and convenience.

It is no secret that the layout of a shipping container home is really open. While this is nice in a lot of ways, there are also some drawbacks. Windows and privacy are two of those drawbacks.

You want to make sure that you place your bed, and your dressing area, away from the windows. It can be hard to know just how much of the inside can be seen, so to test this, go outside when it is dark with all of the lights on in the house, and you can get a visual for how much any passerby can see if they happen to glance over.

All about the wall.

As we have said before, when you run out of floor space, head up. Many television sets and other functional things can be hung on the walls these days, and there are so many things you can put on the floor in their place.

Don't be afraid to hang as many things as possible. It is aesthetically appealing, as well as functional, and you will be happy with all of the floor space you open up.

Visual space says it all.

There is something to be said for visual space. You don't need to have walls to have rooms, and you don't need to have hallways to make it look like you have corridors. What you need to do is place your furniture so it is not all up against the wall.

Place chairs and couches in the middle of the room, or coming out away from the wall. This will give the illusion of a room when there is no wall around. The same can be done with an area rug and some shelves for a hallway appearance.

You may need to practice at this, but it is really an easy way to do things, and you don't have to worry that you will need to build more walls or buy more dividers, your eyes will do it for you.

Over and under.

While the ceiling makes for a great place to keep things, so does under furniture. Who says you can't keep something under the couch if it keeps it out of the way? Coffee tables are another frequently overlooked space.

Slide anything you like underneath them and enjoy all kinds of new free space, and you don't have to worry that you are taking up more room on the walls.

Less is more, and lighting helps.

One of the biggest tips for those who are living in a small space is to be choosy with what you are bringing home. Sure, it is your house and you should be able to decorate it like you would like to, but there are all kinds of things you may be tempted to bring home when it would be better to be happy with what you have already.

As a rule of thumb, keep it simple, and keep it light. There is such a thing as too much, so learn that less is more.

Functional furniture, a lifesaver in a small space

Futons, hideaway beds, and bunk beds are just a few of the ways you can save space in your home. They make all kinds of beds now that are over desks, couches, and futons, making even more options for those who are trying to keep it simple.

There really is no way you can go wrong with a bed you can put away during the day, so keep your eye out for furniture that is more than just a couch.

Multi-Container Homes

You would be surprised at how much different it is when you are working with two units as opposed to one. Sure, you might think that it will open up all kinds of space, but you need to take into consideration the layout of your home, as well as how well you are using that space.

If you have two container homes stacked one on top of the other, then you have to decorate a lot differently than if you have the two side by side. There really isn't a universal law when it comes to multiple container homes, as you can build them however you want them to be.

There is a lot of freedom in this, but you have to keep in mind that it does come with its challenges as well. An optimistic attitude is the best way to deal with any potentially stressful situation, and you are going to end up with the home you want in the end.

How separate is separate?

When dealing with multi-container homes, you need to ask yourself how separate do you want to go. Do you want to make separate rooms, or make bigger, more blended rooms?

The good news is that the choice is yours, but that is a decision you need to make when you are starting this project, and you need to decorate accordingly.

Vertical verses side by sides.

If you have multi-level, we recommend you make the top more livable and the bottom more functional. The whole thing is still your house, but you can make it cozier upstairs this way, and more functional downstairs.

If your containers are side by side, we suggest that you go with the method of making rooms bigger and more blended. This will make it look like you have more space, and make it feel bigger.

Multi-person multi-unites.

Of course if you are living with another person you are going to want to get their input on where and how you keep your rooms. If you are living with a roommate, we suggest that you use more than just room dividers as this will give more privacy and make it easier to be sharing that space.

Room versus storage: making the choice.

There are times when you have to ask yourself if you want a space to look at, or use the space for storage. There is nothing wrong with either choice, but there are times when it is a choice that has to be made.

Stacking boxes and leaving them behind something such as a room divider will make a lot of storage, but then again if you don't want to have that place closed, you may need to consider being more selective with your things.

Getting the pets on board.

All paws on deck. There is no reason that you can't have decorative pet dishes. These are things that are going to be out in your home all the time, so you are going to want to enjoy looking at them.

Plenty of department as well as pet stores have options to decorate with your pet's dishes, and what makes it even better is that you can make them match each other and the rest of your décor.

Watch those windows!

It can be tempting when you are putting in windows to add too many. Windows provide so much natural light, which looks great when it comes to shipping container homes that grab onto the light so much anyway.

But you have to realize the more windows you have, the more you are going to have to work to keep up privacy, and the more you are going to have to clean them.

Laying out your layout.

There may be times when you are moving into a shipping container home, but it isn't one that you built yourself. If this is the case, remember that you need to go with the layout of the home.

Decorate to compliment, and don't put things in places that they don't belong. When you see a room, you can tell if it flows nicely or not. If your room doesn't, then move it around until it does.

Two in one, making the most of furniture.

Any time you can combine furniture, go for it. Loveseats work out better than couches and chairs, as they are almost a combination of the two. Use swivel barstools that will face the kitchen, or living room, depending on where the action is.

Consideration conservation.

Shipping container homes are noisy with all of the metal and usual hardwood floors. Yes, they are gorgeous, but do what you can to minimize the noise and be considerate of your roommate and your neighbors.

Any sound that you would normally think was loud, is about 3 times louder in a metal container, so be mindful of this when you plan your activities about the house.

Ventilation and keeping it fresh.

These small spaces can become stuffy and stale if you are not careful. Keep the windows open and keep fans blowing, for a fresh scent, wax burners are a great option.

Choosing the Look that you want

Design is an integral part of any construction project, especially in a home. The right design can showcase the personality of the occupants at a glance while still being functional and practical.

Generally, there are two ways to design a structure: to **impose** it upon a landscape, or to let it **embrace** the landscape. Depending on the future homeowner's preference, each method will produce a stunning home within a comparable budget.

Embracing the site comes with restrictions on the design. That being said, taking the environment into account and using it to ones' advantage has its perks. A home that makes use of natural lighting and natural buffers against the elements (like forests) will need significantly less heating and cooling, which means less expense.

Imposing a design has the advantage of having more freedom with the actual look of the structure. The home can have the exact detailing that future homeowners want, and can better accommodate any specific needs or demands. However, it requires a more active heating and cooling system.

In the end, preference will dictate the design. With shipping container homes, the possibilities are limitless. This is part of their appeal and the reason why more and more architects and homebuilders are coming up with designs for shipping container homes around the world. This new trend is an avenue to showcase unparalleled creativity and innovation.

With so many options, deciding on which direction to go can be a bit overwhelming. To help narrow down the field, here's a list of a few design options to choose from. They don't even need to be mutually exclusive. Don't be afraid to mix and match ideas!

The Industrial Look

For shipping container homes, this type of design is a shoo-in. Their structure naturally lends them to this kind of style. Their geometrically defined rectangular shape is great when unmodified and shows the clean, simplistic lines characteristic of this style.

The interior as well, is easily done to this style. For example, the corrugated steel walls are usually covered with drywall, but cleaning them up and repainting them (or keeping them bare) is actually a great design statement. This is best done for sections of the wall, functioning as accents, rather than for all of the walls.

Stacking It Up: Multi-Levels

One of the greatest advantages of using shipping containers as a building material is that they are modular and naturally very stable when arranged or stacked against each other. This opens up many possibilities in terms of design.

The result is the creation of multi-level shipping container homes that are not only expansive and spacious with great square-footage, but also eye-catching and architecturally interesting as well. There are so many ways to arrange these containers into exciting shapes and structures; the possibilities are limited only by the imagination.

However, don't forget to make sure that the design is structurally sound by having it examined by professional architects and engineers.

Going Big

Because they are easy to arrange and stack, as previously mentioned, it is actually a simple matter to create a relatively large structure from multiple containers.

In 2010, a French architect named Patrick Partouche designed a home with 2,240 square feet from several shipping containers. This is only one example among many that exist today. Outside of residential projects, shipping containers have been used to build shopping malls and Starbucks shops!

For an expansive home, with spacious living areas, going big is the best choice. And as a bonus, building a big home from shipping containers costs much less than conventional construction of the same scale.

Going Small

If a big home is too much of a commitment (or a little over-budget), then it might be a great option to downsize and go smaller. This is especially true if only one or two individuals will occupy the house. A functional home can be made with two or even just one shipping container. It will be enough for basic necessities and utilities. Some resorts even offer converted shipping containers as their private suites and cabins.

Additionally, starting with a small project is a great way to get familiar with the building process. Before starting on a shipping container *home*, it might be good to get a feel of the build by trying for a shipping container art studio or guest house first.

Eco-friendly And Natural

There are probably few applications of the "Reduce, Reuse, Recycle" motto that are more radical than converting a used shipping container into a house. It is the ultimate display of commitment to environmental conservation. Not only does this recycle the used containers, it also gives them a vital purpose that will keep them useful for many, many years to come.

A good number of shipping container homeowners *are* environmentally conscious, and this has affected their decision to go ahead and build their homes in this way. Some have taken the next step and made their homes even more eco-friendly by relying on solar power, having rainwater collection systems, using recycled materials as furnishings, and more.

The "look" of the house can reflect the commitment to nature and the environment as well. Designs that integrated reclaimed wood, sustainable bamboo, and recycled metal are not at all uncommon for this type of construction.

Making It Fun with Color

Vibrant, loud colors can add a touch of whimsy to *any* structure, but especially to shipping container homes.

Since the shape of the structure itself is already unique and quirky, adding a pop of bright color can bring that extra element of fun to a shipping container home. It's a great attraction for kids and those who enjoy a youthful and energetic vibe.

Some homes have little to no structural modification on the shipping containers, but a splash of color is enough to turn an old steel box into an inviting, fun and unique retreat that showcases the personality of the occupants.

Not a Container House at All

For homeowners who are fans of the traditional style, it is perfectly possible to build a shipping container home that looks like the average, conventional residence.

With the right design and modifications, a shipping container home will look indistinguishable among the houses of an urban suburb. If that's a little *too* plain and ordinary, these materials easily lend themselves to a touch of creativity and modernity that will elevate the home from being just the average "normal" house.

Prefabricated and Mobile

There are people who are not at all picky with design and would prefer a quick build with minimal problems and uncertainties. For these individuals, a prefabricated shipping container home may be the best option.

Many companies these days sell prefabricated homes that are easy to build and will be up and running as functioning houses within days or even hours. While, not custom, these designs still look very appealing and are homes to be proud of.

In addition, many of these prefabricated options are also mobile, so for people who travel a lot and are always on the go, this may be the perfect alternative to a conventional home.

Experimental Architecture

Because the concept of shipping container homes *is* still relatively new, designers are still testing the limits of this type of architecture. There are many outlandish and truly avant-garde styles out there, and for adventurous potential homeowners, this may be the perfect option.

For a truly one-of-a-kind, boldly experimental look, present the challenge to a skilled architect or engineer. Should they be up to the task, this collaboration can result into a completely striking home design that has never been seen. A house like this will be an automatic conversation piece for whoever enters it.

Container Home Interiors

In the end, the second-most interesting aspect of your container home is how you have designed and organized the interior spaces for the most comfortable and functional living. The second most interesting? Yes! The first and most interesting aspect of a shipping container home is that you built it yourself!

The interior of your container home can fully reflect your personality, your preferences, your hobbies, your preferred styles, color schemes, types of furniture and so on.

If you have always dreamed of living in a mountain cabin with wood paneling in every room, here's your chance. If you have always dreamed of living in a steel and glass modern structure, again, here's your chance!

Do you love secondhand furniture because of its lived-in look? Do you need cushions everywhere ... or are wood chairs your thing? Is it restful to you to have bookshelves loaded with books on all walls, or do you relax better with empty walls that have a restful color of paint?

And if you have a double-decker interior – what's your preferred way to get to the upper level?

Inspire yourself with plenty of pictures! If you can do a thing in a traditional home, you can do it in a container home – but why would you? Change things up!

Decorating the Smaller Home

One of the key things to consider when decorating a smaller home is the need to give the impression of space. In order to do this, try to pare things down to the bare minimum. This does not mean minimalist (unless you like and want to rock that particular look) but it does mean keeping things simple whenever possible.

Windows

A larger home might suit heavily decorated windows with voile curtains to permit light in without allowing people to stare into your home, heavy drapes to insulate the home and create a black out in the evenings together with decorative pelmets and swags.

All of these accoutrements which look decorative and striking in the larger home can be overwhelming in a smaller space. In really small rooms consider using blinds instead of drapes (keep all cords secured out of reach of young children), these sit close to the window and do not intrude too much into the room. For use in bedrooms where young children or those who are light sensitive are sleeping it is possible to purchase close fitting blinds that block out all exterior light.

Doors

Where possible consider getting rid of interior doors. Obviously you will still want a door to the bathroom and bedroom for privacy but removing the doors to the living area, kitchen (if regulations allow), office etc. allow light to shine through from one room to another and can contribute to a feeling of space or openness.

Decorations

Just because you are living in a smaller space does not mean that you need to eschew pictures or art on your walls. Choose your subjects wisely, however, and do not be tempted to place too much on any one wall or in one room. Make sure that the colors in the pictures compliment the colors scheme in the room it is hung in and keep to one or two pieces per wall.

Consider hanging mirrors on the walls, these reflect ambient light and therefore help to add to the feeling of space and airiness.

Furniture

Larger pieces of furniture can be overwhelming in a smaller space. Luckily it is possible, these days, to buy many clever designs that optimize the use of the space that you have. Instead of a traditional 3 seater couch, consider purchasing a smaller 2 or even 1 ½ size alternative. Consider the locations of all your furniture so that they are placed to give an illusion of space. Try to avoid, where possible, placing everything against the wall. Use rugs to add splashes of color and decoration to your rooms; it is possible to get striking rugs in all sizes.

Bedroom

Most couples like to have a bed with a walkway on both sides but in a smaller home this may not be possible so look at whether it can be pushed into the corner with a wall light for the person on that side and a shelf in place of a bedside table. By pushing the bed to the side in this way you may find that you can fit a closet or a desk against the other wall.

Designs for Living in Comfort

Almost no one buys an existing shipping container home – at least not yet (but give the market another 10-15 years and some will undoubtedly be put on the market for sale).

Almost everyone, in other words, builds and designs their own container home, or has one built from a customized design that they are closely involved in creating.

If you are building your shipping container home yourself and with friends and family, and have little to no construction experience, never fear: YouTube is here! Those who have built tiny homes or shipping container homes have often video-documented their construction from A to Z for us all to learn from.

If you are a newbie, this also bears repeating: look on the Internet for shipping container designs and plans. You can purchase shipping container plans or blueprints over the Internet. There are also interior designers as well as architects with specific shipping container home experience who are able to provide a customized blueprint that you can take away to build on your own. Again, you can Google these professionals and find some for your region. Simply call them up and ask them how much they would charge for a 30-minute consultation so that you can get your bearings and decide whether you need them or not.

This also bears repeating: Don't launch your construction project without a plan! If you have a creative mind, and your spatial intelligence is fairly strong – you may create the plan yourself. After all, humans have been building habitations and other kinds of structures for centuries, so there are many models you can use and copy to achieve your end goal. However you create that blueprint, make sure you have it on paper with clearly defined measurements.

Since you are having this home built or building it yourself, why not get it designed to perfectly suit how you live in your space? This does not have to be like a property developer project, with every home being designed with the same sized rooms and amenities, in the hopes that it serves the most people. Your interior design can serve you and how you live – and it does not have to please anyone but you!

Creating comfort in a living space is about knowing how you define comfort. Creating functional spaces is about knowing what activities you would like your home to house.

1. How will you live in this container home?

Here are some potential answers:

- "It will be an indoor-outdoor space, while being warm in winter and cool in summer."

This may mean you create a home with huge double-paned windows and window-pane sliding doors, and pay special attention to wall insulation. But it could mean that you want to leave all doors and windows constantly open.

- "We just want a hideaway from town noise. A couple of comfortable armchairs with ottomans; very comfortable bed; shelves for all the books we bring; good natural and electric light. No TV or computers! No heavy cooking!"

This may mean a single-container studio design or a simplified "hotel room" layout. But it could mean that you do glorified camping.

- "I'll take the boys up there in fishing season. That's it."

This can mean that you just need bunks for 8 people and a large grill under an awning, and an outdoor shower setup. But it could also be that you trick out the interior space as a very modern but cozy cabin full of all your city-house amenities.

2. **What functional spaces do you need in your new container home – in other words, what did you build it to achieve?**

Here are potential answers:

- "Beds for six people including children's bunks; galley kitchen and small sized refrigerator; inside hot water shower and toilet; outdoor covered deck large enough for two picnic tables."
- "I need to do water catchment. I need off-grid."

Dual or Multi-Purpose Furniture and Installations

Many container homeowners, and even professional designers, get stuck in the ways that traditional homes are laid out (traditional room dimensions, plumbing and HVAC installations, common window and door placements and shapes) and furnished, (traditional bulky furniture like three-seat sofas, dining room tables with six chairs around it, etc.), but soon come to realize that the traditional home interior design doesn't work for a container home very well. This is for a number of reasons, some of which are obvious.

Among the obvious reasons:

Not all container homeowners wish to have traditional ceilings and traditional floors installed.

Not all container homeowners were ever content with the layout of their traditional homes! It seems that they are confused at the "odd" interior design of most traditional homes that never seem to respond to any modern life functionalities.

Here are some ways space can used to gain the maximum usage of your new container home interior. Some are "design" ideas, while others are "utilities" oriented.

- When you look at the "tight interiors" of the smaller container homes and even at the larger container houses, you can be reminded of yacht or ship installations, where every inch is used wisely – to fulfill one, two or more very clearly-defined functions…like the kitchen carousel designed for boats (again, there are dozens of ideas to be copied from boat and yacht interiors):

- Choose furniture and storage solutions that are dual or multifunctional:

- Storage under staircases, as pullout drawers or open shelves for books, shoes, tools, kitchen pots and pans or dishware, etc.

- Each bed and bunk, every chair and seating bench has storage under or inside it.

- An outdoor shower set within a wide concrete pillar, which also serves to hold up one of the ends of an upper story container cantilevered above it.

- Even a "ceiling" can be multi-functional: Use metal grate walkways instead of a solid ceiling for your lower-level container, with skylights as the ceiling for the corresponding upper-level container. The metal grate walkway can be an actual hallway on the upper unit, or simply a part of the floor of that space.

- Consider 12-inch high windows tucked ceiling-high the length of the container, and that slide open laterally. As they bring in lots of natural light and air, they take away the "boxed in" feeling of being inside a containerized space. You will also benefit from more mid-wall space for shelves or cupboards that are within your easy reach.

- Alternatively (or simultaneously), use clear roofing materials or skylights, placed above highly functional spaces of the home (e.g.: above the kitchen work counter; over the stairwell, in a bathroom/shower ceiling, etc.).

- Consider commercial sun/rain awnings – fixed or mobile/retractable – to cover your outdoor patio or deck on the sunny side of the home to help keep the interior cooler in hot weather. Mobile ones are easy to roll up or remove in winter when you welcome the warmth of the sun into your home.

- Build 12-inch deep / 12-inch wide drawer cabinets, instead of the standardized 18-inch deep and 21-inch wide drawers – so that you do not narrow down your walking spaces in (for instance) the kitchen or bathroom areas.

- Use Japanese-style interior sliding doors to create movable privacy modules (with translucent or semi-translucent panels, decorative or plain, to let light pass through both areas).
- You also gain the space a laterally opening door would take up in that room.

Heating solutions:

Use radiant under-floor heating coils in utility rooms and entry floors; install heated towel rods in bathroom and kitchen. In many climates, this can create more than enough heat for your home ... or at least a room.

Put heaters (HVAC systems) high on a wall, rather than along baseboards; place outlets higher on the wall as well – this is so that you have the option of bolting shelves, drawers, furnishings at and below waist height.

Use a heating module that detects human movement (the Japanese are said to have invented these) – you place it high on a wall and it rotates the blades so that the heat blows toward you when you enter or move about the space.

Go for height and light – place a 10-foot container on top of your main living area – cut out the lower container's ceiling and upper container's floor for a 2-story ceiling; put skylights (or clear roofing material) in the roof of the upper container. Light and height opens the feel of the space.

Hinged fold-down/fold-up table surfaces, stored upwards or downwards into any wall– they can be placed in a reading nook or next to a bed, in the kitchen as food-preparation countertops or dining surfaces, etc. They can also be temporary shelving when placed higher on an open wall.

Install water catchment gutters and barrels around the outer roof edges of the home. Divert the water to irrigate your kitchen or flower gardens, or to supply an outdoor (or even indoor) shower.

Landscapes – Grass Sod Roofing

This can be as much a functional addition to your home as a beautifying one. The sod can insulate; whatever you plant in your roof garden can beautify.

One-Function Container Rooms

What are some of the single-function living areas you can create with any size of container? Sleeping rooms & living rooms as separate containers with common area connecting halls. A spa or pool house space. A gardening cabana. A resting place for a cool drink next to your private tennis court. A backyard gazebo. A treehouse retreat.

And all from shipping containers.

Saving the Space for Last

While it is true that not all shipping container homes are small-sized or even approach the "tiny" designation, why not build into your design some fun space-saving or otherwise multipurpose functions that mimic small-home economies of space?

While it is also true that most shipping container homes are designed from A to Z to come in at much less than $50,000, even doubling that budget keeps all owners well under the majority of traditional home purchase prices. Why are we mentioning this? Because you can let yourself go a little crazy and creative with a few "designer features". The designer features will really individualize your home, and many of them are dual- or triple-purpose features that help you save space, should your container home be one of the smaller designs.

Truly, the biggest challenge for most people who are reading this will be to think outside the traditional home layouts. Thinking differently about the traditional interior spaces confuses most people, since they have mostly lived in traditional interior spaces! Thinking differently about a kitchen requires a little bit of an imaginative stretch when all you have known is the usual "upper plus lower cabinets, hole for the fridge and double sinks" layout. If you just can't imagine "spaces" – and spatial intelligence is a skill that not everyone has, so don't feel bad – for a few hundred dollars, you can consult an interior design specialist. Almost all of these designers today use computer-assisted design (CAD), and they can mock up some options for you on a computerized presentation. They will include some images of furniture, add a few different color schemes, and even put some items on your CAD walls, so that you can get a real sense of how the space can be lived in. For all those of us who don't have that spatial intelligence, this is a very exciting way to see the interior of your container before committing to any design.

If you are one of the lucky few who can visualize how spaces can be tricked out and furnished, go for it – but remember that you can still hire an interior designer or architect to create a blueprint of your very own design.

A blueprint is a map with precise measurements of how everything fits in and around your shipping containers. You will want even a rough blueprint that you yourself have created before you begin any work on your new home. In the end, it will save you money, time and frustration – because it will prevent you from making errors that you need to spend money, energy and time to correct.

The Art of Minimalism

Because most shipping container homes are quite small, you will want to maximize the space within them. Even though you want to simplify and minimize the amount of space you are working with, you still want your home to be as functional as possible. To follow are three tips for maximizing the square footage in your beautifully quaint shipping container home.

1. Build a Loft Space.

In most conservative-sized shipping containers the bed is the feature that occupies the most square-footage. For this reason, many homeowners who decide to live in this type of abode choose to construct a small loft space directly above the main floor. This loft space can be made up of a second shipping container, placed atop the primary container located at ground level. By simply placing a ladder on a diagonal, you create a means of moving from the main level to the loft. By creating a loft space you open up the pathways on the main level of your home. In so doing, you are also making an economical decision because the heat from your main level will rise and thus keep you warm and toasty at night.

2. Introduce Build-in Furniture

Another way of maximizing the space within your shipping container home is by way of built-in furniture. On this note, built-in furniture comes in a wide variety of shapes and sizes. Perhaps you are a homeowner who is hoping to downsize, but who nonetheless possesses a larger number of books. If these books are your treasures, and you cannot stand to part with them, you will need to store them in an economical fashion. In order to do so, you will want to install built-in bookshelves that lie flush with the rest of your home. This is a decision you will need to make before purchasing your shipping container home, so that alterations can be made accordingly.

Another great idea for built-in furniture is that of incorporating a pull-out dining room table. This dining room table can be positioned just under your kitchen counters, and can easily be installed to tracks: Allowing you to pull it in and out with ease. Purchase a few backless stools that can similarly be stored underneath your kitchen counter, opening up your kitchen for more enjoyable cooking and eating experiences.

Storage Solutions that Add Space

Clever furniture and storage solutions can really make the difference when you are living in a smalls pace.

Kitchen

A smaller kitchen is likely to have limited counter space so take the time to think about the appliances that you use most often. It may be possible to get a number of them, i.e. ovens and microwaves built into the wall. Look at smaller appliances to fit into your mini space.

It is possible to purchase half size dishwashers that fit into a fraction of the space of the normal size ones. If you do not have a utility consider purchasing a European style front loading washing machine and installing it, British style, under your kitchen counter. If you do not have access to a garden to dry your clothes consider purchasing a combination washer dryer. Many microwaves now do double duty as a grill and an oven and can be used in place of a counter top sterilizer to clean your baby bottles. If you are really stuck for space a traditional stove top kettle will boil almost as fast as an electric one and look pretty stylish doing it!

Living space

Try to make as much of your furniture do double duty as possible. A coffee table can come with integrated storage space; your couch can be a pull out. Don't forget the vertical space – put up shelves to store books, DVDs etc.

Consider whether you use your television and DVD player set up on a regular basis. If so does your television need to be so large. A smaller house will need a smaller screen as you will, of course, be sitting closer to it and many models these days come with an integrated DVD player so there is no need for a separate console. Consider mounting the television on the wall to free up the floor space that would otherwise be taken up by the console. If you watch a lot of your media online you may even be able to get rid of the television all together in favor of streaming your viewing through a projector and onto a wall or pull down screen.

Dining area

If your kitchen area is large enough you may be able to install a breakfast bar or a kitchen table. Alternatively in some smaller homes the dining area is in the living room.

Many families that live in smaller homes eat on the couch in the living room but there are real family benefits to be gained from sharing a meal. Luckily this is possible even if your space is limited. You can purchase a small, folding table. With chairs that collapse and slide in underneath. It is the act of moments to open up the table and set out the chairs. Sometimes a house is large enough to permit half the table and chairs to be kept out at all times with the other half being opened up when guests arrive. Look for furniture that works for you!

Entrance

In many smaller homes the entrance opens straight into either the living area or the kitchen. Place a mat immediately by the door so that guests can clean their shoes and have a rack for shoe and umbrella storage. A set of coat hooks are useful, one per person to avoid over cluttering. Keep one seasonally appropriate coat per person in the 'coat area' with all others being stored in the closet.

It is useful to keep a small desk with a key tray and a place to put a handbag. This means that these items do not clutter up the rest of the home.

Bedroom

If space is really cramped consider installing wall lights in place of bedside lights and putting up shelves instead of bedside tables. Some beds are designed with a shelf in the headboard for this exact purpose. Many beds are designed with under-bed storage options and this can be a handy place to store out of season clothing, heavy bedding or larger items such as suitcases. It goes without saying that suitcases should never be stored empty – they are the perfect protection for your winter quilts!

Closet

There are no end of inventive closet solutions to maximize your space, from hanging shoe racks to hangers that hold double the normal amount. The best advice is to invest in vacuum pack storage bags, store all out of season clothes in the bags.

Children's rooms

Children have a lot of junk; they also need a space that they can call their own in order to allow them to feel secure.

Luckily children love bunk beds. If your family has to share a room, bunks are an optimum solution, put shelving on the wall so that they can keep their own treasures in their private space. You can even put a tent up over the higher bunk and curtains around the lower one to give each child their own area. For children who have their own rooms a bunk style high sleeper can still prove very useful, the child sleeps high giving more space under the bed for a desk, closet, play space or toy storage.

Guest rooms

Do you really need a guest room? Only you can answer that but it is probably useful to have a pull out cot under a bed in one of your children's rooms or a pull out couch in your living space. If you do have a guest room, think about making it work for you all those weeks of the year when your guests are not visiting. Guest rooms make perfect places to store books or a home office.

Layouts and Innovations

Look around for transformable dual-purpose furniture, such as a sofa that transforms into a pair of bunk beds – in the exact same floor space the sofa had just occupied. This is interesting in small spaces, as the bunk beds will take only the floor surface that your sofa uses.

If you use fold-down tabletops, don't waste the wall space by simply folding up the tabletop against the nude wall. Make a frame with narrow shelving (up to 4 inches deep, as an example) for which the hinged tabletop folds up and locks to become the door.

A free-floating designer sink with open (uncovered) plumbing pipes, for instance, may cost much more than your miniature RV-style sink and even more than your standard kitchen or bathroom sinks – but if budget is not an issue and you wish to have fun with some designs that are off the beaten path, why not go that route?

Let's look at more ways to use the space in ingenious ways that you just may never see in a traditional home.

Multi Levels on One Floor

Create different living levels in one container – a sunken living room, or a raised sleeping or study area. No carpeting, as you should also install trapdoors in the raised floors that lift up and give access to the hidden storage. Add drawers at the front of the raised floor that pull out into the main room so that you benefit from more storage, accessible anytime with ease.

Staircases

Steel staircases, circular or not, can still store books or shoes and other small knickknacks through hanging shelves (or hanging rods or hooks) off the back of each step.

Use the back of higher steps as a hanging rod for clothing (coats and jackets) on hangers or install hanging hooks for clothing.

Make a pet bed under your straight-line staircases – this is a great "nook" type of indoor space to train your pets to go to overnight or in bad weather.

And don't forget the now-world-famous Harry Potter Cupboard under the Stairs storage room. Ask any child how to make one!

Clean and Dirty

Make half of your single-container garden shed into a neat and clean living or relaxing reading area, while the other half houses your muddy tools and equipment. This is great if you plan a kitchen garden of any size and know you'll spend hours at a time some distance from your home. Your garden books are right there where you need them, along with your seeds, your tools and all the rest.

More Storage: Drawers

Drawers don't necessarily need to pull out laterally. Place a drawer vertically in a countertop. As you pull the drawer upwards to access it, it automatically locks in the fully up position. You can design the interior of the drawer to be open on both large sides and crisscrossed with spice rack (or other purpose) shelves accessible from both sides.

For easier access, get some shelves in your cupboards that pull out like an open drawer – most will come with a locking mechanism to lock it to the distance you pull it out. This creates a bigger and more practical shelf usage – you never struggle to reach something stored way at the back of the shelf. Upper-level cupboards and lower cupboards can benefit from this type of installation.

Just like we do with stove/oven units where it is built in, transform the baseboards under your lower kitchen cabinets and the dead space behind them into pullout drawers. Make them as high and deep as you can, of course, but also make them much wider than any other drawer (up to 3 feet across). They should be high enough to store cutting boards, flat oven pans or over-sized serving platters – yet still very accessible. In other parts of your home, you can do this to store linens and foldable clothing or even footwear that is out of season.

You can adapt the above suggestion to hold dog or cat food and water bowls. Pull the drawer out, and your pet can eat and drink, push it in and their bowls are out of the way while you are using the floor space to do other things. Just remember: empty the water bowl before you shove the drawer back in!

Speaking of pets: If you have an indoor cat, consider hiding its cat box in a lower cupboard. The cat has a permanently open "doggie door" on one side of the cupboard to enter and leave; you have a normal door in front so that you can easily pull out the litter box for cleanup. It can be an under-counter hiding place, and be located in virtually any room of the house.

Racks

Use of accordion drying rods over a sink or a tub – they simply push back into the wall. Place them high enough so that you can still use the shower or tub when the rods are pulled out. You can also use a framed and hinged drying rack, which folds up out of the way against the wall and down to dry clothes.

Likewise in your kitchen, you can install wooden window blinds on fold-down hinges, with the blinds serving as a drying rack for towels and lightweight clothing. HINT: The blinds are on a swivel installation in the frame.

If you live outdoors quite a lot around your container home, think of installing a knee-high shower hose outside the door you use to come back into the house. Also install some grid shelves or a small metal baker's rack next to the shower hose, on the outer wall, to store and dry off wet boots and footwear you have just hosed off. Gridded shelves or metal racks allow for excess water to run off, so you can also just hose down your footwear once it is on the shelf.

Seating

If you have a bar seating area at a countertop, use industrial-grade swivel mechanisms that allow backless bar seats to fold under the bar when not in use, while swiveling out to a perfect distance for comfortable seating.

Entertain a lot? Use stackable ottomans for extra seating. Design your staircase for seating.

Don't forget the beauty of skylights, as they can open up your container home to Mother Nature and help it feel more spacious. Don't worry that an open skylight creates too much heat or light – almost all skylights come with light-blocking canvas or other synthetic materials as sliding shades.

Transform any sized table into an under-tabletop storage nook. Just think of a pool table with its higher sides, supporting an actual tabletop. When you want to play, you remove the tabletop. When you want to eat you put the tabletop back over the ledges. Adapt this concept to create storage (of any depth you choose), and you have gained space for all types of large and small items that you don't use on a daily basis. If it is a large table, imagine it with 2 or 3 sectional tops, or a roll-back mechanism.

Everyone has heard of Murphy beds. However, most of the time, Murphy beds are conceived and installed to require a clear and clean floor space underneath them. Who wrote the rule that it has to sit 6 to 12 inches off your floor? This is not very practical when you live in small spaces, especially when you have other furniture or furnishings on the floor space the opened Murphy bed requires. What is the solution? Install the twin, full, or any size Murphy beds higher on your wall so that it naturally sits well above any other furniture that you might use in your space. Remember that container homes are 9 feet tall inside. You can adjust the bed installation so that the Murphy bed sits at the height of a sofa back. You can adjust it so that the bed sits above any tabletop (or on it, if you agree to be neat and empty the tabletop in order to use it as a support for the bed itself). Get creative with height!

Organizing Small Spaces

The amount of space you have is more perception than anything because you are only ever taking up the space of your body. You could become claustrophobic in a mansion given enough shadows and yet a canal boat can feel infinite. One of the key tricks is to open space up as much as possible, either by making things as open plan or by creating the illusion of space. You can do this with long mirrors or windows (and in shipping containers you can make these windows very big) but there are other, less intuitive, considerations. Opting for small blinds instead of tent-like curtains or picking light wooden-frame furniture, with space underneath, instead of heavy and blocky couches will let you see more room, even if you can't ever use it.

While many people choose to live in shipping container homes for the novelty of it, there are many others who choose to do so because it really does cut down on waste for what ends up in the landfills.

These people tend to be ambitious in many ways, and aren't about to stop at the fact that they are living in an upcycled home. There are too many other ways you can recycle and reuse what is around you!

Here are some ideas that involve recycling things you may have no need of anymore, or upcycling those things you find in a second hand store.

Tennis shoe flower pots.

Tennis shoes make great flower pots. Simply drill a hole in the bottom, fill with soil and seeds, and you are ready to go. This is a fast and simple way to bring a bit of quaint into your home.

Ladder shelf.

Ladders are good for more than just standing on. With a bit of mounting hardware, you can lean a ladder against the wall, secure it in place, and you will have yourself a perfectly new shelf that can be used for a number of different things.

Wall china closet.

Hang your plates on the wall when they are not in use. This is an easy way to store your dishes, and make a fun and interesting decorating scheme on your wall.

Use dishes that are in line with the current season, and have easy decorating all year round.

Door bookshelves:

Try building a doorway into a bookshelf. There is the fun mysterious look to this as it looks like a hidden room, and you have a lot more storage space. They are surprisingly easy to make, and all you really need is a book shelf, doorknob, and hinges.

Boxes on the wall.

Box cadies are perfect shelves to open up space on the floor. Simply mount these against the wall, and you have two new shelves, instantly, as well as floor space underneath.

Shelves in the cupboards.

Cupboards save a lot of space as is, but when you add shelving to the back of them, you open up that space even further. Line all of your lower cupboards with shelves, and you will be amazed at how much more you can fit inside of them.

Entertainment Studios.

Entertainment centers can be converted into so many different useful objects. Place them in the kitchen for a place to store your pots and pans, or put them in the laundry room for all of your laundry needs.

Paint them to fit in wherever you need them, and you can have one for every room.

Feeding a small army.

Stack your cans in alphabetical order in your cupboards. So many people lay them side by side, but they really take up a lot more room that way. Make sure you are stacking them so you know what they are inside, and you will be amazed at how much more you can fit into your cupboard.

Hollow hallows.

Hollow boxes that double as tables or storage boxes really do a lot for fashion and function. You can put several foot rests at the foot of your couch, and each of those could be a storage space for something else.

It is a great way to keep things within reach, but out of sight as well.

Mason jar candle lights.

Try using tea lights in mason jars hanging from the ceiling for a fun and homey way to bring light to your evening. It brings a cozy and comforting feeling to your home, and if you use scented tea lights, you don't have to burn your melted wax that day!

Chapter 6: Maintaining your Shipping Container Home

Cleanliness is everything

One of the things you'll need to get used to in a small space is that you will need to clean up more; the previous small pile of clothes in the bedroom corner could become the clothes that are now your bedroom floor. To prevent this from happening too much you will need to avoid owning too much stuff that could get left out on tables or the floor but you can also design your home so that you don't have to clean up as much, such as in built clothes hampers or storage space. This will only allow you a minimal amount of things that can cause you are problem.

Small Home Mindset

You use 20% of your stuff 80% of the time. The trick, therefore, is to make sure that you know what that 20% is and what, of the other 80% you really do use from time to time and what is just junk. Be strict with yourself, your wardrobe, your kitchen, your books and DVDs, what do you really and truly need. You will surprise yourself.

Before moving into your smaller home you will need to declutter your life, we have tips and strategies to help manage this in the next chapter but a small home mindset is about more than decluttering – you need to make sure that, once you have moved in, you do not start to fill up your beautifully designed small space with stuff that you buy. When you go to the store and see that steam mop your friends have – do you really have to have it?

Decluttering is the key

Clutter is the enemy of small spaces because they just cannot live together and accommodate you as well. This means avoiding too many ornaments that could be in the way but also opting for walls that don't have too many pictures or bulky decorations on them and keeping the furniture down to what you need. There are ways to do this while still having pictures on the walls; you could choose to have a digital frame, you could create a collage instead of one large picture, you could use lots of smaller photographs on places like the fridge or by choosing to rotate a few pictures as the year goes by. The fewer items you have closing in on you when you sit in a room the more room you will feel in their place.

Room by Room

Go through your home, room by room and make an inventory of any large furniture items. What do you have? Will it fit in the new place? Is it a family heirloom or does it have sentimental value?

Once you have a list of the larger stuff you can decide what to do with it. If you are very fond of an item but it will not fit in your new place you will need to loan it to family or friends or arrange for a storage container to house it. If you do not have a sentimental attachment to the item, consider selling it, either at a yard sale or on craigslist or similar listings. The money you earn can go towards buying new items.

Now that you have a plan for the larger items you can go through your smaller bits and pieces.

Books and Media

Some people sell or pass on books as soon as they have read them, others like to keep a library with them at all times. If you are one of the latter types you will need to think about what you can do with your books. Work out how much shelf space you will have in the new home (don't forget that you can put shelves all the way up to the ceiling) and keep only the books that will fit on those shelves. The remainder should be stored or sold.

Invest in an e-reader such as a Nook or a Kindle. This will allow you to keep your books with you at all times, the feel of an e-reader can never physically replace the feel of a good book but you will get used to it.

As mentioned earlier move as much of your media as possible into online storage that can then be streamed to your television when you want to use it.

Kitchen

Many cooks love their gadgets but smaller kitchens just cannot accommodate everything. Do you really need a bread maker, rice cooker, ice-cream maker and separate toasted sandwich, muffin and cake –pop machines? They might all be nice to have but how often do you really use them. Most of the functions of these machines can be done by something else, you toast sandwiches in the toaster or grill and bake muffins, bread and cakes in the oven. Rice can be cooked quite successfully on the stove.

In the same way think about how many pans you need – while it can be lovely to have a specialist pan for jam, soups, casseroles etc. think about investing in a good quality multipurpose set. You only need as many pans as you have burners on your stove!

Sell as much as you decide you do not need and invest in multitasking gadgets that will help you maximize your new work space and a good set of stacking storage containers.

Clothing

The best time to organize your clothing is at the turn of the season. As you are coming to the end of winter look through your wardrobe and put aside any winter clothing you have not worn over the past few months. Ask yourself whether you wore it the year before and if the answer is no it is time to eBay the item if it is a designer item that has held value or send it on to the thrift store. Perform a similar exercise with handbags and shoes.

Do not get so enthusiastic that you get rid of all your special occasion wear – this should be looked at separately! Once you have performed this exercise you can send the expensive items to the drycleaners, wash and iron the rest and put it all into vacuum bags for easy seasonal storage. Do the same with your summer and transition wardrobes.

Be quite strict with yourself, you only need two sets of towels and two sets of bedding per person (one in the wash and one in the bathroom), some people even manage to get away with one set per person, washing and drying them in the same day!

Kids' Stuff

It can be tempting to store a lot of your kids' stuff either for sentimental reasons or in the hope that they will use them for their own children.

While it can be heartbreaking to get rid of the clothes your much adored children wore as babies you really only need to keep one or two items for sentiment, their coming home from hospital outfit, christening gown, first shoe etc. Pass the rest on to family members who can use them or to the thrift.

The same thing should be done with toys. Keep the toys your child plays with or ones that will genuinely be used by a younger sibling. Keep their special comforts but get rid of the rest – far better another child can enjoy them than they sit in your storage unit for years.

Repeat the exercise for kids' furniture. If you had a very high quality cot or crib it might be worth keeping but bear in mind that safety standards change and your kids might think that you want them to put your grandchildren in a death trap. Unless it really is very nice (and try asking a friend to give you an unbiased opinion), pass it on to someone who will use it now!

How to Pass It On

There are a number of different ways to pass items on, some of which can net you a fair bit of money on the items you no longer need. Whatever method you chose to use make sure that you wash and clean all items beforehand, nobody wants to buy something grubby!

Many areas will hold a regular yard sale and these can be a brilliant opportunity to get rid of the stuff you have decluttered without having to drag it anywhere. You might even make a fair amount of money for it, don't be tempted to set your prices artificially high, if something you have priced high is not selling accept a lower offer, you will save money on storage costs!

Online sites such as Craigslist and eBay are a fantastic way to offload items. EBay is particularly useful for popular items that will hold their value such as high end prams, maternity clothing, designer wear and handbags etc.

Thrift stores will often be happy to take your donations, you may need to deliver clothing to them but many will arrange to collect bulky items. Do not forget to ask places such as care homes or schools whether you have anything that might be of use to them. Board games (homes for the elderly), toys (schools and daycares), books and DVDs (everywhere) are often very gratefully received as donations.

Maintaining your Container Homes

There is so much excitement that goes with decorating your own space, especially when you have the freedom to do what you want with it. You do have to keep in mind, however, that there are things that just don't work.

There have been a lot of ambitious people out there, but some of the methods that people have tried to do when it comes to these homes just don't work, no matter who you are or how creative you can be.

Here are some things that you should avoid because they may cause harm to your shipping container home, or because there are better ways to do it. You are free to express yourself, but we want your home to be the best it can be.

Everything Has Its Place

'A place for everything and everything in its place' is a saying that you will probably have heard from time to time. It may, initially, seem like hard work to put something away every time you have finished using it but it will truly help you to manage your home.

A smaller house quickly becomes overwhelmed if too much stuff is left out. That book you were reading with your coffee? Put it back on the shelf and wash out the cup before going to get the groceries! Those clothes you were wearing today – the ones for washing should go straight into the laundry basket with suits or other 'wearables' being hung up neatly not strewn over the back of a chair. Any kitchen appliances that are not used on a regular basis should be washed and put back after each use – if not you will find yourself bemoaning a lack of counter space when in truth you have plenty.

Kitchen Storage

One of the advantages of a large house with a big kitchen is the fact that you can keep a fully stocked larder full of staples to hand at any time you need them. You can still run a larder in your smaller kitchen you just need to make sure that you organize it properly.

Clever racks and pivots can turn corner cupboards into rotating racks perfect for storing tins and it is easy to buy full height pull out larder drawers that fit perfectly next to your fridge. Check out the options and solutions in your local kitchen design store.

The key to managing a compact larder is simple. Keep the stuff you use all the time in the center shelves and towards the front with items that are used less often on the top or bottom shelves and towards the back. Group items by type and you will easily be able to pick out everything you need. Invest in good quality stacking storage boxes, they will help keep your ingredients fresh, look clean and will help you make the most of the space you have available.

Filing

There are so many papers we all need to keep to hand, bills, bank statements, and medical records. Wherever possible go paperless, your records will be stored electronically and can, if necessary, be printed out as and when required for the IRS or loan applications.

For items that you need to keep safe and to hand purchase a small file that will fit under your bed or in a drawer. Keep a year's worth (or the minimum you can get away with) there. All your key documents such as passports and birth certificates should be in a fire safe lock box or, if you do not need to access them regularly, at the bank. Keep scanned copies of all documents on your computer (with a backup on a computer of a family member in a different location in case of fire).

Digitize as much of your media as possible – these days Netflix and other similar services have made it increasingly unnecessary to purchase physical copies of films or TV series.

Ornaments and Pictures

Ornaments and pictures make a room but too many can be overwhelming. Try to keep a few on display and store the others safely in the loft or a small lock up if you rent one, you can always rotate them round from time to time.

If you have kids you know that they bring 'art' home on a regular basis and each piece needs to be displayed. There are a few options here and you can probably think of more. You could have one item per child per week to be displayed on the fridge door. Alternatively you could hang a pin board in the kitchen or on the doors of their rooms and allow them to display the art work of their choice, binning the 'used items as and when they want. Another solution is to photograph each item of art as it comes home then, once a year, create a photo book of each child's work. These books are typically quite small format but can become fabulous heirlooms as time goes on, they could even make a great Christmas gift for a doting grandparent!

New Stuff

As mentioned earlier in the chapter, do try to think about whether you really and truly need a new item before you purchase it. If you do decide that you need it think carefully about where you will store it. If nowhere suitable springs to mind what can you move, sell or junk in order to make the space available? If you can't house it do you still need it?

External Storage

While an attic or basement would be an ideal place to store you're out of season items (Christmas decorations, seasonal clothing etc.) or furniture that will not fit in your new, compact, home you may not have the luxury of this space. Most towns and cities will have secure storage units available for rent. If you have items that you need to keep but will not fit in your home consider renting such a unit – it will make your life much easier on a day to day basis and help to remove a source of stress.

Don' t skimp on the services.

When you first move into your home, make sure you bring in the professionals to do the plumbing and the wiring. A lot of people think they can do it themselves, and only end up causing problems for themselves later on.

This is your real house, so you want all of these services done the right way.

Make sure you do your homework.

Research the cost of one of these homes, as well as well as your projects before you begin. One common complaint a lot of people have is that they didn't realize how much these homes cost initially.

Do your homework and budget so you know what you are getting yourself in to.

Placement is key.

If you are placing your own home, make sure you do it in a smart place. A lot of people think they can put them anywhere, and while they can go more places than a traditional home, they still have standards.

Always ask yourself if the placement of your home is safe and practical no matter what time of year it is.

Windows are made of glass.

The big windows people place in these homes are gorgeous, but they are also huge sheets of glass. This is something that you will want to keep in mind if you have small children, as well as when you are trying to decide where to place your home.

Too close to anything that could potentially hit it, and you could be dealing with a lot of money in damages.

Keeping your cool when it is hot outside.

These metal homes can get really hot, especially in certain times of year. Keep your fans on and your windows down, and if you are feeling really fancy, invest in an air conditioning system.

Keeping them cool can be a challenge, but it is well worth it.

Don't over plan the work, or the plan.

In short, be flexible. Things are going to come up and other things may not go as planned, but that isn't the end of the world. Keep an open mind, and work with what you have to work with.

Don't get bogged down with all of the little details, you are making a house a home, so this ought to be a fun time for you.

Be mindful of the neighbors.

Don't build too close to the neighbors. Again, with the open floor plan, you might find that you are on display if you are not careful. Place your home in an area that gives you privacy, and if you are putting in your own windows, choose the placements with the neighbors in mind.

Use the proper tools.

These are massive steel containers, which means you will need to use special tools if you are drilling into the outside of them for any reason. This can be done, but you want to be sure you know what you are doing.

Be safe and be smart, and only use tools that are suitable for the job.

Keeping it clean.

Shipping container homes are smaller, but this doesn't meant that they need to be cluttered. Make sure you do what you need to do to keep your home clean on the inside and outside.

If you don't put siding up on the outside, make sure you keep an eye out for rust. This is your home you are going to be living in, make it the best it can be.

Managing for life.

Upkeep and maintenance are key when it comes to any home, and these homes are no exception. Make sure you do your part to keep your home and yard up to date and clean, and that you do all of the maintenance that you need to do to make it last.

You and everyone who sees your home will love it for years to come if you take care of the little things right away.

Additional tips to remember

Shipping container homes are practically weather proof but this does not mean that they will last forever. It is important that you know how to maintain and care for your shipping container home so that you will end up increasing the lifespan of your container homes. This chapter will discuss the care instruction of your shipping container homes.

- Always check for leaks and apply rubber caulk immediately. Unlike concrete homes, shipping container homes are made from steel and the presence of moisture can lead to corrosion and rust over time.

- Regularly apply a fresh coat of weather proof paint on the exterior. This is important in order to keep the exterior walls of your shipping container home protected against different types of weather conditions.

- Avoid installing a flat roof as well as parapets because this can increase the problems related to maintenance issues. You can put earth bags on the roof especially if you will cover the shipping container yard with another roof. This will provide better insulation from the roof and will prevent too much heat from entering your house from above.

Taking care of shipping containers is not that difficult. All there is to it is to check for the presence of cracks and deal with the problems as soon as possible.

Shipping Container Homes, Dos and Don'ts

To follow are some of the leading dos and don'ts to abide by when it comes to both building and decorating your shipping container home. Keep these tips in mind as you move forward with this wonderful and life-changing venture.

Dos

If you decide to move forward with building your own shipping container home, to follow are some of the steps that you will absolutely want to follow.

1. Do take stock of your furniture. Do the same with your accessories. Once you have done this once, take a few days off and consider these belongings a second time over. Once you have done so, you can develop a better understanding of how to organize your home.

2. Do be bold. Often when homeowners begin to build and decorate their quaint shipping container homes, they feel that they need to be conservative in the doing. While you will want to create a cohesive aesthetic in this smaller space, you need not shy away from bold color and prints.

3. Do pay attention to the exterior of your home. Far too many owners, of shipping container homes, end up focusing almost exclusively on the interior. It is quite important that you spend an equal amount of time and attention on the exterior of your space. Failing to do so will fundamentally reduce the value of your home.

Don' ts

When building your shipping container home, you will want to absolutely avoid doing the following:

1. Do not take on too much. Many people believe that they can save on both materials and labor by doing all of the major renovations on their own. If you do not know how to install sliding doors, or how to operate a crane, do not attempt to learn on this project. If you take on too much, you will likely end up needing to spend even more money on botched materials that need to be replaced.

2. Do not clutter. As has been mentioned, one of the main reasons that homeowners appreciate shipping container homes is for how they encourage minimalism. Therefore you will want to catch yourself anytime clutter begins to collect. One way of doing so is by evaluating whether an item is essential or superfluous.

3. Do not rush the process. Building a shipping container home is an incredibly rewarding process; however, it is also a process that you will not want to rush. Take a few months to fully plan the design, layout and construction of your house. If a project—like creating openings—is not going as smoothly as anticipated do not try to rush through it. Consider wrangling more help, but do not risk ruining any or all of your hard work. On the whole, building your shipping container home in full might take up to four months. This is a realistic timeframe to work within-keep this in mind as you move forward with the construction of your shipping container home.

Conclusion

Building a house or structure using a shipping container is a very fun and rewarding thing to do. Aside from being economical, using shipping containers and upcycling them to become posh and functional homes is very friendly to the environment. It is a trendy fad that many people are trying to adapt and you should too.

You can add your own personal touch to any of the ideas that we gave you, and make them truly your own. No matter what you want to do with the space that you have, it can be done with a little bit of know-how and some good old fashioned hands on work.

If you can picture it, then you can build it, and make it whatever you want it to be. Don't let anyone discourage you or tell you that you can't make it the way you want it to be, this is your home, and it should be exactly what you want. If there is a way you can make it homier to you, then you should do it.

Printed in Great Britain
by Amazon